OUTBREAK

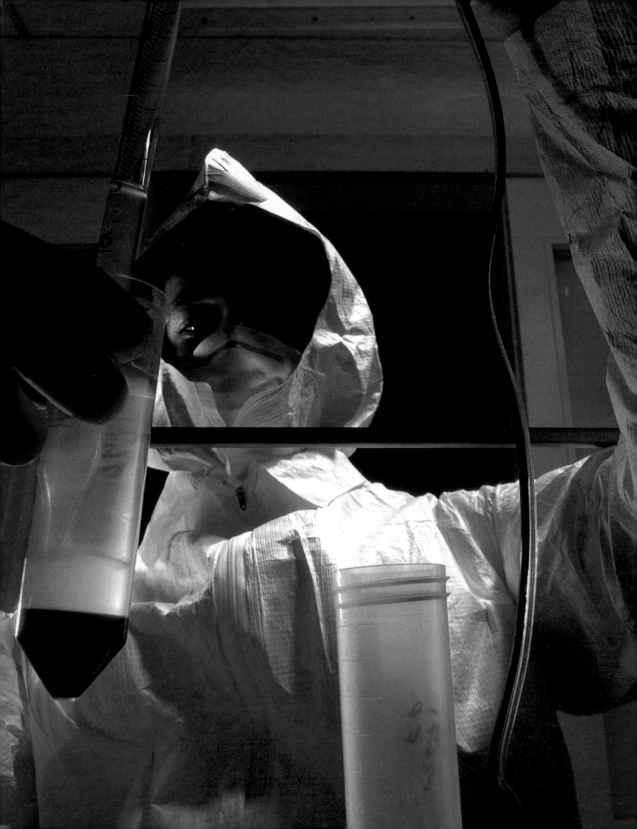

OUTBREAK

disease detectives at work

Mark P. Friedlander Jr.

UPDATED AND REVISED
Third Edition

Twenty-First Century Books ■ Minneapolis

Dedicated to Dorothy

I wish to honor the memory of Leonard T. Kurkland, M.D., Ph. D., Professor Emeritus of Epidemiology, Mayo Clinic, who generously reviewed the original manuscript, offered helpful direction, and wrote the forward.

Page 2: A researcher in protective clothing removes human immunodeficiency virus (HIV) from a culture for testing.

Twenty-First Century Books
A division of Lerner Publishing Group, Inc.
241 First Avenue North
Minneapolis, MN 55401 U.S.A.

Website address: www.lernerbooks.com

Library of Congress Cataloging-in-Publication Data

Friedlander, Mark P.
    Outbreak : disease detectives at work / by Mark P. Friedlander Jr.—[Rev. ed.]
        p.   cm.—(Discovery!)
    Includes bibliographical references and index.
    ISBN: 978–0–8225–9039–2 (lib. bdg. : alk. paper)
    1. Epidemiology—Juvenile literature. I. Title.
    RA653.5 .F75 2009
    614.4—dc22   2008025277

Manufactured in the United States of America
1 2 3 4 5 6 – BP – 14 13 12 11 10 09

CONTENTS

FOREWORD

This book provides a history of epidemic infectious diseases, such as the plague, smallpox, influenza, Ebola, and AIDS. It introduces the student to epidemiology—the study of disease occurrence in populations. Epidemiology is not the same as medical care of patients. The epidemiologist, or disease detective, looks at medical care in an entire community or country as a source of epidemiologic data. These data may include the description of a disease—how old are the people who are affected? Do more men or more women get the disease? What are their jobs? The data may also show the geographic and seasonal distribution of cases—whether the disease happens in just one city, state, or region, for example—or whether it strikes only in summer.

The essence of epidemiology involves understanding a disease and its causes. This involves three main steps. First, a physician describes and records what he or she has observed, including the symptoms of a disease. Second, laboratory tests help develop a specific diagnosis, such as "German measles." Finally, the epidemiologist compares the characteristics of people who are affected by the disease with those of people who are not affected.

The science of epidemiology began with the battle against infectious diseases such as smallpox and influenza. Early in the twentieth century, epidemiologists successfully extended their methods to include conditions such as mercury poisoning, vitamin deficiencies, and hormonal abnormalities such as diabetes and goiter. In recent decades, epidemiologists have studied diseases such as cancer, heart disease, and stroke. The result is a better understanding of how these disorders work and a clearer path to identifying their causes and treatments.

This book is a tribute to many of the clinical investigators and epidemiologists who have conducted studies at universities and at centers such as the Pasteur Institute in Paris, France, the National Institutes of Health in Bethesda, Maryland, and the Centers for Disease Control and Prevention in Atlanta, Georgia. Students will learn about critical public health questions and their solutions through epidemiology. Some who read this book will become the scientists who identify and control risk factors for diseases of the future.

Leonard T. Kurland, M.D., Ph.D.
Professor Emeritus of Epidemiology
Mayo Clinic
Rochester, Minnesota

INTRODUCTION
The Blue Men

On the morning of September 25, 1944, a ragged old man was carried by ambulance to the Beekman-Downtown Hospital in New York City. He was a homeless man who had passed out in the street and was in a state of shock. Most remarkably, the man's nose, lips, ears, and fingers were sky blue—a beautiful but unhealthy color.

After being treated in the hospital, the man began to recover. The blue turned back to the healthier pink. The doctors suspected gas poisoning—but where and how? Before the day was over, ten more elderly homeless men were brought to the hospital—and all were bright blue.

The hospital called in the chief epidemiologist, or medical detective, of the New York City Department of Health, Dr. Morris Greenberg, and another department epidemiologist, Dr. Ottavio Pellitteri. One of the blue men died that night, but the others seemed to be recovering. The doctors at the hospital and the epidemiologists began to realize that these cases were not gas poisoning. As the men became well enough to answer questions, it became clear that the only thing they all had in common was that they had eaten breakfast at a local cafeteria,

In New York City in 1944, a number of men fell ill with a mysterious ailment that turned their skin bright blue.

(9)

the Eclipse, a place where homeless and poor people could get cheap meals. Each man had eaten oatmeal, rolls, and coffee and had fallen sick within half an hour of the meal.

The doctors suspected food poisoning, but the onset of illness had been sudden for each victim. This was not typical of food poisoning. Could it be drugs? Blood tests showed that none of the men had used drugs.

When the doctors went to the restaurant to investigate, they found filth—roaches, flies, old grease covering the kitchen walls and ceiling, garbage on the floor mixed with dirt, and leaking sewer pipes—but none of these had directly caused the illness. In addition, the cooks reported that they had fed more than one hundred customers at breakfast that day, and no one else became ill.

Dr. Greenberg and Dr. Pellitteri gathered samples of everything that was used to prepare the meals the eleven homeless men had eaten: ground coffee, sugar, evaporated milk, rolls, dry oatmeal, and salt. The cook explained that he had used 5 pounds (2.3 kilograms) of dry oatmeal mixed with 4 gallons (15 liters) of water and a handful of salt to make oatmeal for the customers. He showed the scientists the can of salt he had used. Next to that can was another can that looked just like it.

When Dr. Greenberg looked into the second can, he realized that although it looked like salt, it wasn't. Instead, it was saltpeter, or sodium nitrate, normally used to make corned beef and pastrami. Still, this could not have poisoned the men.

Dr. Greenberg and Dr. Pellitteri took the samples back to the Health Department laboratory. To their surprise, they learned that the can that they thought contained sodium *nitrate* actually contained sodium *nitrite*. Both substances look and taste the same, just like table salt; but sodium nitrite is a mild poison.

The homeless men's symptoms fit the picture of sodium nitrite poisoning. But there was still another puzzle. If sodium nitrite had been in the oatmeal instead of salt and more than one hundred people had eaten the oatmeal, why had only eleven men become sick?

Then Dr. Greenberg remembered something from his youth. While most people put sugar on their oatmeal, some older people liked to sprinkle salt on theirs. He and Dr. Pellitteri went back to the cafeteria to check out the saltshakers. There were seventeen shakers, one at each table. Sixteen shakers contained salt. One contained sodium nitrite.

Although the eleven men had not eaten at the same time, they had all eaten at the same table. They had all sprinkled extra "salt" on their oatmeal—just enough sodium nitrite to give them the blues.

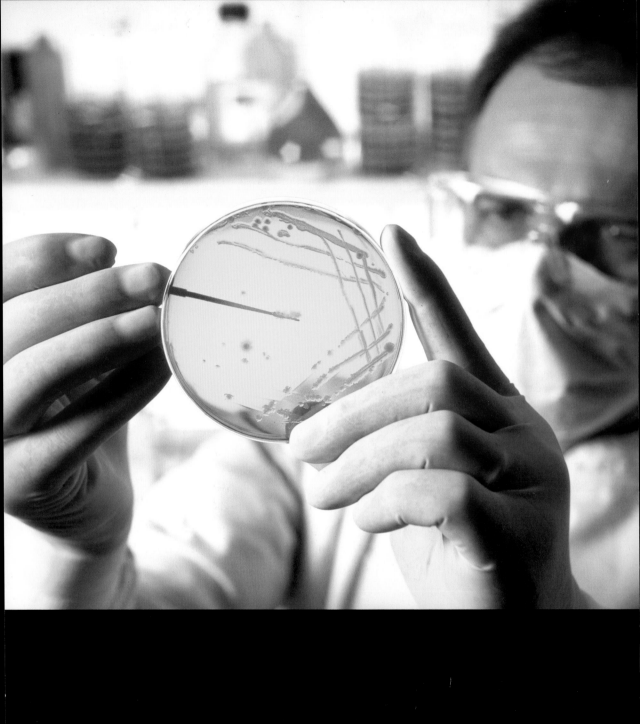

CHAPTER ONE
Epidemiology: The Study of Disease

- *Over half the passengers on a cruise ship in the Caribbean Sea come down with severe diarrhea.*
- *An eruption of tuberculosis sweeps through a Los Angeles high school, infecting one-third of its students.*
- *Thousands of people in Milwaukee suddenly become ill from drinking tap water.*

These outbreaks of illness were epidemics. An epidemic is an unusually high number of cases of a disease among a group of people. An epidemic disease that spreads throughout an entire country or continent or the whole world is called a pandemic. (Sometimes, however, even a massive pandemic is referred to as an epidemic.) AIDS is a pandemic. Some epidemics or pandemics develop slowly, and other outbreaks are sudden and unexpected.

Epidemiology is the study of the distribution, identification, and nature of health and disease. While physicians treat and study health and disease in individuals, epidemiologists look at health and disease in a population. Epidemiologists' areas of study include chronic diseases such as cancer and heart disease; infectious diseases such as the flu or measles; reproductive, maternal, and child health; nutrition and health; violence; injury

A masked researcher examines lines of bacteria growing in culture.

prevention; genetics; aging; and disabilities.

Infectious disease epidemiology, a major focus of this book, is a core field within epidemiology. Infectious disease epidemiologists focus on the incidence, distribution, and control of infectious diseases—those that can spread. These epidemiologists hunt for the causes of diseases that affect populations and try to stop the spread of those diseases. Infectious disease epidemiologists are disease detectives.

Many diseases that produce epidemics are caused by microbes—microscopic organisms—that cause contagious, or infectious, diseases. Microbes include bacteria, viruses, parasites, and fungi. Microbes spread disease by traveling through the air and in water, bodily fluids, and food. Diseases may spread from animals or insects to humans, or from person to person through contact with bodily fluids (for example, droplets produced by coughing and sneezing). Thus, the disease detective must search not only for the cause of an epidemic disease but also for the means of transmission—how it spreads.

You have probably read about the devastating epidemics of the past, such as the plague, which destroyed one-third of the population of Europe during the Middle Ages. But epidemics are not just something from days gone by—they still affect people all around the world. Some epidemics, such as AIDS, are massive. Thanks to the work of epidemiologists, many modern epidemics have been contained, or stopped. The work of these men and women is often slow and difficult and sometimes dangerous.

(THE BEGINNING OF EPIDEMIOLOGY)

In 1830 a rumor swept through London, England, that a deadly and unknown disease was spreading from India to the

United Kingdom. At the time, the United Kingdom controlled India as part of its widespread British Empire. Most people in London paid little attention to this rumor.

Many poor citizens in London lived in filth and squalor. The streets were dirt and mud. Garbage and human and animal waste ended up in the Thames River, the source of most Londoners' water supply. Other waste seeped into the common public wells around the city. People drank, cooked, and washed with the same water into which waste was dumped. As the population grew, the water became even more polluted, but most people did not worry about how crowded and dirty the bulging city had become. By 1832 the new disease, cholera, was not just a rumor in London but a terrible reality—an epidemic.

Cholera is caused by a bacterium, *Vibrio cholerae*, that can survive for long periods of time in water. When a person swallows water containing cholera bacteria, acid in the stomach may kill the bacteria. But if the bacteria survive the stomach acid, they move to the intestines, where they multiply rapidly. The person may develop sudden and violent diarrhea, vomiting, and fever, followed by death. A cholera victim's dehydrated body shrinks into a shriveled skeleton, and the skin turns black and blue. Death from cholera is often dramatic and swift.

Thousands of different types of bacteria exist all around us. Bacteria are single-celled organisms that are usually encased in a rigid cell wall. Some can move using hairlike cilia or long, tail-like flagella that stick out from their bodies. Most bacteria are harmless—and many are beneficial, such as those that live in our intestines and help us digest food. But bacteria that produce disease, such as *Vibrio cholerae*, can be very dangerous. They release toxins (poisons) that cause damage to their host. A host may be a plant, insect, animal, or human.

In the early nineteenth century, no one knew that diseases were caused by microorganisms, or germs, such as bacteria and viruses. These tiny organisms are invisible to the naked eye. It wasn't until the late 1800s that scientists began to understand that germs cause disease. But even in the early 1800s, only a few doctors believed that dirt and filth bred disease, although they did not know why.

A British doctor named John Snow was one of those. He guessed that dirty water held the key to the spread of cholera. In 1848 Dr. Snow began collecting records of cholera deaths, noting where the most deaths occurred and who supplied water to those neighborhoods. At the time, eight water companies provided water to different parts of London. Dr. Snow noticed that cholera rates were highest in areas where the water was supplied by two companies, the Lambeth Company and the Southwark and Vauxhall Company. These companies both drew their water supply from the sewage-filled Thames River.

When a wave of cholera cases swept through the Golden Square neighborhood of London in 1854, Dr. Snow began to keep more detailed records of deaths. He became more and more convinced that the cause of cholera was in the water.

Next, he went from house to house in a neighborhood called Soho, where many people were dying of cholera. He asked many questions. He learned that the people who had died had drawn their water from a public pump at the corner of Broad and Cambridge streets. He guessed that the water at the Broad Street pump was causing the disease. But he also found out that ten people who lived closer to other public pumps had also gotten cholera. This fact cast doubt on his theory.

Dr. Snow visited the families of those ten victims to get more information. From them he learned that five of the ten had

Many poor Londoners in the 1800s lived in filth and squalor. The field of epidemiology began when Dr. John Snow investigated the source of a cholera outbreak in the city in 1854.

been going to the Broad Street pump because they thought the water tasted better, and three of the victims were children who attended a school near that pump.

On September 7, 1854, Dr. Snow met with city leaders. He revealed his findings and requested that the Broad Street pump be closed. Some officials laughed at his theory. What good would it do to shut down a water pump? But since no one else had a solution or a cure for the deadly epidemic, the city officials agreed to remove the pump handle. The epidemic subsided in that area of the city.

Following his success with the Broad Street pump, Dr. Snow broadened his study of cholera deaths. He determined that there were nine times as many deaths in areas where water was supplied by the Southwark and Vauxhall Company as there were in areas supplied by the Lambeth Company. While Southwark and Vauxhall drew water from a very polluted part of the Thames River, the Lambeth Company had switched its water source to a less polluted section of the river. From this data, Snow concluded that cholera was caused by polluted water. He had begun the art and science of studying epidemics and is considered the "father" of epidemiology.

(MODERN EPIDEMIOLOGY)

The modern science of epidemiology involves much more than studying sudden outbreaks of disease. Microbes are not the only cause of disease within a population. Too much cholesterol in the diet can lead to heart disease. Cigarette smoking within a population can result in an increase in the number of cases of lung cancer.

The evidence that supports the connection between a cause, such as smoking, and a disease, such as lung cancer, is referred to as a statistical association. Not all smokers develop lung cancer, and nonsmokers also suffer from lung cancer. But statistics show that more smokers than nonsmokers develop lung cancer. This relationship, or association, is important. For an epidemiologist to make a valid statistical association of a disease and a cause, he or she must analyze the makeup of the group that is affected. Who is getting the disease? Is there really an association between the assumed cause and the disease itself, or is the observed association a matter of chance?

Suppose, for example, that the number of cases of AIDS in the United States increased by 6 percent over a given time, and during that same period, the value of the stock market also went up 6 percent. Because the percentage is the same, there would appear to be a statistical association between the increase in AIDS and the increase in the stock market. But the growth of the stock market wouldn't have anything to do with the spread of AIDS—the 6 percent rise would be simply coinciden-tal. A statistical association alone is not enough to determine the cause of a disease—there must be some biological mecha-nism that could cause the disease.

Dr. Gary Friedman, an epidemiologist and author of a text-book on the subject, outlined another example of a false asso-ciation for disease. He asked this question: Is a man or woman who has had a parent die more likely to suffer from back pain than a person whose parents are still alive? He found no rela-tionship between the death of a parent and low back pain for people aged 30 to 39. On the other hand, 84 percent of his re-search subjects between the ages of 50 and 59 who had at least one parent die did suffer from low back pain. When he grouped the statistics from all subjects from age 30 to 59, the data ap-peared to show that parental loss was related to low back pain.

But this result was nonsense. Dr. Friedman had not ac-counted for another factor, or variable. Men and women aged 50 to 59 are more likely to have had at least one parent die than people aged 30 to 39. Also, people in their 50s are more likely than people in their 30s to suffer from low back pain. The pain is most likely due to the aging process—it has nothing to do with the death of a parent. Still, when the statistics concerning people in all age groups from 30 to 59 were combined, they showed that more people who had a parent die have low back pain than do those whose parents are still alive. The results were not scientifically valid, because of a false association that had been introduced by the ages of people in the study. Epidemiolo-gists call this false association confounding. In this study, age was acting as a confounder of the association between death of a parent and back pain.

By gathering statistical data according to carefully framed

rules, epidemiologists can determine the relationship between a disease and its possible cause. Epidemiologists use what is called a cohort study to establish the risk of getting a disease. A cohort is a selected population of people, such as all the residents of a community or all the customers who ate hamburgers at a certain restaurant within a given time frame.

(THE ROCHESTER EPIDEMIOLOGY PROJECT)

For decades the Mayo Clinic, a large hospital in Rochester, Minnesota, has kept health records for people living in the region. These records provide precious information for epidemiologists.

In 1907 a Mayo physician, Dr. Henry Plummer, began keeping detailed medical records about people living in the city of Rochester and surrounding Olmsted County. Thirty years later, Dr. Joseph Berkson developed a more elaborate index system, using a three-digit code to keep track of the records. Then, in the 1960s, a young doctor named Leonard T. Kurland realized that these medical records represented an epidemiological gold mine. He saw that he could build a database for population-based studies of the causes and outcomes of disease.

Since the records covered a long period of time and a specific region, epidemiologists could study diseases that occurred in this population to calculate how often a certain disease could be expected to occur naturally in the population at large. This would help doctors to know if the number of cases of a particular disease was higher than average within a certain group of people. For example, by studying the Mayo Clinic data, scientists might learn that a disease such as meningitis (inflammation of the tissue that envelops the brain and spinal cord) occurs naturally at a rate of one case per year among ten thousand people in the United States. If eight or nine cases suddenly appear within a short period of time in a community, then the researchers would suspect that a specific event or mechanism might be causing the outbreak.

Dr. Kurland began his data system, called the Rochester Epidemiology Project, in 1966. At first, records were kept by hand, then on paper tape, punched cards, magnetic tape, and finally on computers. The data provide a baseline to measure the normal frequency of various diseases in a population. This statistical baseline has given public health doctors everywhere the necessary information to sound the alarm when they discover that the incidence of a disease has increased. Hundreds of studies have used this data.

CENTERS OF EPIDEMIOLOGY

Epidemiologists work for universities and public health agencies in cities, states, and countries around the world. The World Health Organization (WHO), an international public health organization affiliated with the United Nations, was established in 1946. It is headquartered in Geneva, Switzerland, and is controlled by the World Health Assembly, made up of the health ministers of 193 member countries. WHO helps track diseases, coordinates global health projects, and provides funds for health projects around the world.

In the United States, the most important public health agency is the Centers for Disease Control and Prevention (CDC) in Atlanta, Georgia. The CDC tracks emerging diseases and epidemics across the nation and alerts state health departments to potential problems. The agency identifies trends in public health and informs and educates people about health problems. It deals with a wide range of health issues in addition to infectious diseases. These include developmental delays, birth defects, school nutrition, and injury, violence, and suicide prevention. But the CDC's most dramatic work happens when scientists from the agency act as a medical "SWAT" team, rushing to the scene of a disease outbreak.

The CDC stores hundreds of thousands of specimens of viruses, bacteria, parasites, and other microbes for reference. Researchers use these samples to determine the cause of a disease by matching the characteristics and shape of the new microbe with those of the stored samples. Microbe samples are first labeled and catalogued and then frozen and stored in negative-pressure rooms. If there is a leak or break in the seals of a negative-pressure room, all air will flow from the outside to the inside, keeping the microbes contained.

When scientists want to test for the presence of a microbe, they place a drop of blood or other body fluid from the infected person in a petri dish. A petri dish is a round, shallow glass or plastic dish filled with a culture of rich nutrients such as agar (a nutrient extracted from seaweed), in which microbes will normally grow and multiply. Scientists look at samples of the new, multiplying microbes under a microscope and compare them with the samples stored at the CDC. The process is similar to that of a detective matching a suspect's fingerprints with samples kept by the Federal Bureau of Investigation (FBI). Scientists can also identify a microbe by a process known as immunocytochemistry, which involves the use of antibodies (proteins that are part of the human immune system) and color dyes.

CDC research labs are numbered as levels 1 through 4, according to their biosafety level. In a Level 1 laboratory, scientists work with ordinary organisms that do not cause disease.

The Centers for Disease Control and Prevention in Atlanta, Georgia, is one of the top research centers in the world.

At Level 2, the work involves microbes that cause mild diseases, such as viruses that cause the common cold or bacteria that cause diarrhea. In a Level 3 lab, the microbes being examined may cause a serious disease but one for which there is a vaccination or medicine available, such as rabies, Rocky Mountain spotted fever, yellow fever, Q fever, Rift Valley fever, or botulism. Doctors working in a Level 3 lab must be vaccinated for the contagious diseases with which they are working.

For the life-threatening microbes for which there is no vaccine and no cure, the work is done in a Level 4 lab—called the hot zone. To enter the hot zone, an investigator must pass through several chambers. In the first room are lockers and a

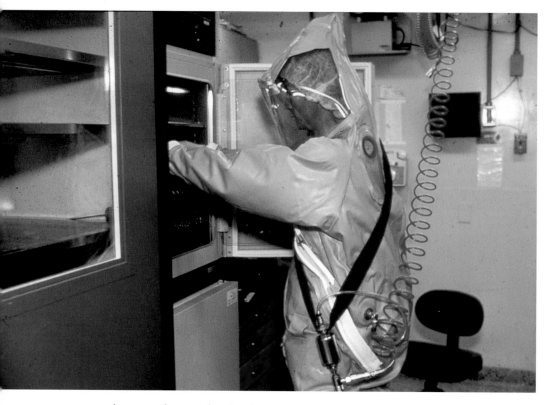

A researcher at the CDC wears a tightly sealed blue Chemturion suit to do research in the hot zone.

dressing area, where workers remove their clothes, shoes, rings, and other jewelry. They dress in full coveralls, taping their sleeves where they join gloves and their legs where they join socks. Next, they don a bright blue "Chemturion suit," a pressurized, helmeted, booted, gloved "space suit." When investigators leave Level 4, they must go through a decontamination shower before removing the Chemturion suit. There are only two Level 4 laboratories in the United States and just a few elsewhere in the world.

CHAPTERTWO
A Closer Look at Microbes

When officers of the Epidemic Intelligence Service—the elite corps of medical detectives at the Centers for Disease Control and Prevention—head to the heart of an outbreak of any new or mysterious disease, they must try to identify the microbe, if any, that caused the disease. Diseases may be caused by many other things as well, such as genetic factors, toxic chemicals, or vitamin deficiencies. But most epidemics are the result of microbes, which are tiny organisms that can be seen only with a microscope.

Microbe and *germ* are words that generally describe microscopic invaders that cause contagious diseases. There are three major types of microbes: bacteria, viruses, and parasites. The most likely cause of an epidemic disease is either a bacterium or a virus. Some infectious diseases, such as malaria and sleeping sickness, are caused by single-celled parasites. Diseases such as Rocky Mountain spotted fever and typhus are caused by a group of bacteria called *Rickettsia*. There are many microbes that spread from animals or insects to humans. Malaria is spread by the bite of a mosquito, for example, and Rocky Mountain spotted fever and Lyme disease are carried by ticks.

(BACTERIA)

A bacterium is a single-celled organism. It may be shaped like a ball, rod, or coil. Hairlike flagella stick out like flowing arms from some bacteria, allowing them to move. Mostly, they travel with the flow of fluids. Like other single-celled creatures, bacteria require nutrients and oxygen, and they reproduce by dividing.

Bacteria cause damage to the human body by releasing chemical poisons. These poisons kill human cells, producing symptoms of illness.

According to Dr. Rita Colwell, a biologist at the University of Maryland who has devoted many years to studying microbes, there are anywhere from three hundred thousand to one million species of bacteria. So far, scientists have identified only two thousand of them.

Many major epidemics have been caused by bacteria. Bubonic plague, or Black Death as the plague was called, killed

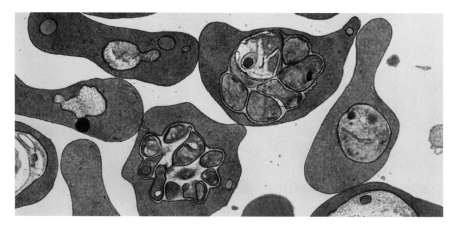

These red blood cells are infected with the parasite that causes malaria. Parasites are multiplying in the two cells at the right. Eventually the cells will burst, releasing parasites into the bloodstream.

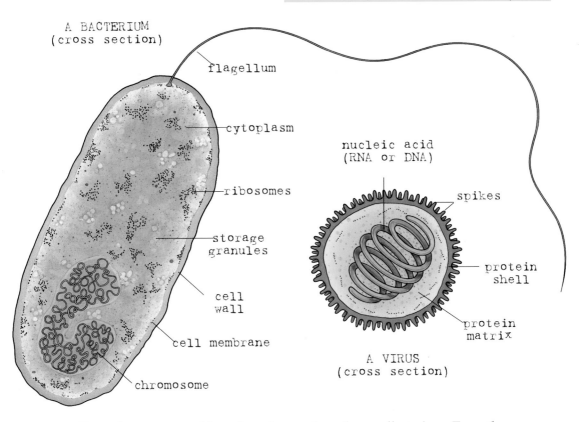

A BACTERIUM
(cross section)

flagellum

cytoplasm

ribosomes

storage
granules

cell
wall

cell membrane

chromosome

nucleic acid
(RNA or DNA)

spikes

protein
shell

protein
matrix

A VIRUS
(cross section)

Bacteria are ten to thirty times larger than the smallest virus. Even the largest virus is only about the size of the smallest bacterium.

thousands of people in medieval Europe. It was caused by the bacterium *Yersinia pestis* and was spread by fleas that had fed on the blood of infected rats. Cholera is caused by the bacterium *Vibrio cholerae*, which lives in contaminated water or food.

Cholera epidemics still happen in places with a limited supply of clean drinking water. In the summer of 1994, thousands of refugees fleeing brutal killing in Rwanda, Africa, crowded along Rwanda's western border. They used the nearby waters for sewage disposal as well as for washing and drinking. The conditions were perfect for cholera bacteria to breed, resulting in an outbreak of the disease. In some areas of South America and India that do not have good sanitation systems and clean drinking water, many people die of cholera. In the United States, cholera outbreaks are rare, but they do occur.

The lung disease tuberculosis, or TB, is caused by a type of bacterium known as a mycobacterium. TB bacteria travel in water vapor particles that are released into the air when a person infected with TB coughs or sneezes. Tuberculosis is a serious problem around the world, especially among poor and homeless people. It is rarely transmitted outdoors in the open air. Most often, it spreads in confined public areas such as hospitals.

Generally, bacterial diseases can be treated by medicines called antibiotics. The most well-known antibiotic is penicillin.

(VIRUSES)

Bacteria are so small that they can only be seen under a microscope. But viruses are even smaller than that—they can only be seen under the most powerful microscopes, electron microscopes, which can magnify objects one hundred thousand times their actual size. If a bacterium were the size of a basketball, then a virus might be the size of a marble.

A virus is the smallest and simplest of life-forms. It is a protein shell enclosing a core of nucleic acid. (Nucleic acids such as RNA and DNA are the molecules in a cell that carry hereditary information and direct the cell's activity.) There are more than fourteen hundred known viruses. They have many shapes, but most are round or cylindrical.

By itself, a virus is totally passive. It cannot eat or reproduce or do anything at all until it gains entry into a host. Once inside a host, a virus locks onto the wall of a cell. The virus finds receptors on the cell surface that fit like puzzle pieces with protein molecules on the surface of the virus. Then the virus chemically drills into the cell, or as some scientists suggest, it is "invited" in. But a virus is a terrible guest. It goes immediately to the nucleus of the cell and forces the cell to become a manufacturing plant to make more viruses. Within an hour, a cell produces one hundred new, identical viruses, which pop out of that cell to attack more and more cells. Within seven hours, a single virus can multiply to a hundred thousand viruses. Some viruses fill a cell and burst out of it, while others bud out onto the cell's surface. A viral attack can bring on disease symptoms quickly. Smallpox, yellow fever, mumps, measles, chicken pox, polio, and flu are some of the commonly known diseases caused by viruses.

(THE DISCOVERY OF MICROBES)

The first person to consider the idea of a microscopic living organism was the Roman writer Varro. During the first century B.C., he suggested that people became sick because they breathed in "tiny animals," or "animalcules," that were invisible to the eye. But it took more than fifteen hundred years before his theory caught on.

The second clue came from a Dutch cloth merchant, Antoni van Leeuwenhoek, who lived from 1632 to 1723. Leeuwenhoek devoted much of his time to his hobby of lens grinding. He hoped to improve the glasses he used to examine the texture of cloth and draperies. As his lenses became better, he began to examine water. He wanted to see if there was any difference between rainwater, well water, seawater, or water from melted snow. What he found was that water contained small, squiggly "things" that no one had seen before. He referred to them as "wee animalcules."

The origin and function of these animalcules remained a mystery until 1857, when the French chemist and medical scientist Louis Pasteur established that diseases were caused by bacteria. While working to understand why some bottles of wine were bitter, Pasteur discovered that bacteria caused wine to ferment (undergo a chemical change). He also learned that he could control bacteria with heat. The process of killing germs with heat is called pasteurization after Pasteur.

During this same period, a German physician, Robert Koch, developed a technique for growing colonies of bacteria. He

Left: *Louis Pasteur discovered that diseases can be spread by bacteria.*

Below: *A nineteenth-century microscope that may have been used by Pasteur*

The German physician Robert Koch was the first person to isolate the bacterium responsible for tuberculosis, a devastating disease that still affects people around the world.

extracted a sugar called agar from seaweed and found that it worked well as a culture medium. The ability to grow large quantities of bacteria enabled him to connect diseases to specific bacteria.

Toward the end of the nineteenth century, scientists and doctors began to accept the germ theory—the idea that infectious agents, or germs, caused diseases. Then, in 1892, a Russian scientist, Dimitri Ivanovsky, made another discovery. Using a special filter called a Chamberland filter candle, which had pores so small that bacteria could not pass through it, Ivanovsky realized that some germs could pass through the filter. These germs were smaller than bacteria. They could not be seen with a microscope.

Six years later, Dutch scientist Martinus W. Beijerinck confirmed this finding. But it was not until 1930, when German scientists developed the technology necessary to build an electron microscope, that people could actually see viruses.

CHAPTER THREE

Great Plagues of History:
Bubonic Plague, Smallpox, and Anthrax

When epidemiologists from the CDC or the World Health Organization race to investigate some new outbreak of disease, they go armed with all the knowledge of modern science. They know to question whether the outbreak is related to a chemical poison or to a disease-causing microbe. They know they must investigate the way the disease spreads. They also know that they must try to find the source of the chemical or the breeding place of the microorganism. Finally, they know they must try to control the epidemic and prevent future outbreaks.

But the knowledge we take for granted has been long and slow in coming. Until the late 1800s, people could only guess at what might be causing the terrible plagues that killed millions of victims. No one had any idea how these plagues spread, how to prevent them, or how to cure them.

(THE BLACK DEATH)

In the fall of 1347, bubonic plague arrived in Italy. Ships bringing silk, spices, and precious metals from Asia sailed to the ports of Messina, Sicily, and Genoa in Italy. As the ships docked at

A 1564 illustration shows Spanish priest Petrus Martinius (right) *and his monks nursing and burying plague victims.*

the piers, crowds came to meet them, expecting to see wonderful new wares and hear exciting stories. Instead, what greeted them was a horror beyond their understanding.

On board the ships were dead bodies and sick and dying men. Their faces were covered with black and blue splotches. Their bodies looked like skeletons. They had grotesque, bulbous growths and pus-filled sores. Although some people in Europe had heard stories about this terrible disease, no one had seen it up close.

The plague began with swelling of the lymph glands in the groin, neck, and armpits. These swellings, or buboes (from which the name *bubonic* comes), grew to the size of an egg. Dark splotches appeared on the skin, along with boils oozing pus.

The wisdom of the time held that diseases were caused by body fluids being out of balance. The doctors called these fluids humors. The term had nothing to do with a jolly mood. According to the theory of humors, the body contained four basic liquids—blood from the heart, phlegm from the brain, yellow bile from the liver, and black bile from the spleen. Doctors believed that when these humors were out of balance, sickness would result. They also believed that certain diseases were caused by poisonous gases that floated up from swamps. They called these vapors miasmas. People built fires or carried bouquets of flowers and sweet herbs to ward off the foul vapors.

Scientists have since discovered that bubonic plague is caused by the bacterium *Yersinia pestis* (abbreviated *Y. pestis*). Fleas bit rats infected with *Y. pestis* and then bit humans. The bacteria flowed in a person's bloodstream to the lymph nodes and then spread to the liver, spleen, and brain, destroying these organs. While the bubonic plague was spread mostly through the bite of infected fleas, it also passed directly from person to person

The port of Genoa, Italy, in the fifteenth century. The Black Death was carried here by rats that stowed away on ships coming from the Far East.

through coughing or sneezing. This pneumonic, or airborne, form of the plague spread rapidly, particularly in crowded cities.

The bubonic plague had originated in Mongolia, a region in eastern Asia. Changes in the climate forced Turkish and Mongolian nomads into new areas in search of food and water. Black rats found refuge in the nomads' caravans, traveling with them westward through India, into the Crimea region of eastern Europe, and to northern ports on the Black Sea, where Italian merchants had established trading colonies. With the rats went the plague, leaving behind a wide swath of death. According to some estimates, half the population of China fell victim to the plague during the thirteenth and fourteenth centuries.

In 1345 the plague struck Caffa, a major trading city on the Black Sea. The citizens were baffled and afraid. No one could figure out the cause of this deadly disease. At the time, the Muslim citizens of Caffa were fighting Christian traders from Italy who had come to buy spices and silk that had been carried overland from Asia. According to one historian, the citizens of Caffa enlisted the aid of a local ruler, Janibeg, to fight the Christian merchants. When the merchants discovered that they were about to be attacked, they fled to a walled fortress in Caffa. They would have been defenseless against Janibeg's army had it not been for the plague—that relentless and nondiscriminating killer. The Black Death struck Janibeg's men as they lay siege to the fortress. In an angry final attack, Janibeg ordered his remaining men to catapult the dead bodies of soldiers over the walls of the fortress where the Italians were hiding.

The merchants fled to their ships to sail home, carrying with them the black rats and the plague. By the time the fleets reached Italy, most of the merchants and sailors were dead or dying. Some ships never made it home—everyone on board died, leaving the ships adrift at sea.

When Italian officials realized that the sailors and merchants were bringing disease to their cities, they ordered the men to remain on board in a quarantine—the enforced isolation of sick people to prevent the spread of a disease. But the rats did not heed the quarantine. They scurried down the docking ropes and brought infected fleas into the cities. The Black Death spread quickly. During the next two years, it moved northward through Europe and across the English Channel to Britain.

In Europe in the mid-1300s, life was difficult. For years, the winters had been harsh, the summers wet and cold. Crop failures and famine were common across the continent. In the countryside, peasants lived in shacks with dirt floors and straw-thatch roofs. They often shared their homes with their farm animals. By doing that, they risked getting animal-borne diseases, such as tuberculosis, influenza, and measles. The cities were crowded and filthy. Inside city walls, houses were tightly packed along dark, narrow streets. Garbage and human waste were thrown into open ditches, which flowed into rivers and streams. Bathing was considered dangerous. Vermin—rodents and insects—were an accepted part of city life.

People who lived in medieval times were no strangers to disease and famine. They were used to fatal and crippling diseases, including leprosy, typhus, smallpox, yellow fever, and malaria. But the Black Death was the most frightening. It struck Europe with tremendous force, condemning both rich and poor. Few people lived more than a week after being struck with the plague. With the pneumonic form of the disease, someone could be healthy in the morning and dead by nightfall.

Neighbors and friends fled from plague victims. Parents even abandoned their children. Victims often had a fever so high that they became delirious. They would shout and gyrate crazily in a final dance people called the dance of death. As the victims died, foul-smelling fluids—sweat, excrement, and saliva—flowed from their bodies. The stench was overwhelming.

Crops were left to rot in the fields. Farm animals, left alone by owners who had either fled or died, wandered the countryside. Wolves entered towns and cities and fought over the corpses festering in the streets.

While some people believed the plague was a punishment from God for man's sins, others blamed Jewish people, who were a minority in Europe. Thousands of Jews were burned alive by hordes seeking vengeance for the Black Death.

Within two years of its arrival in Italy, the bubonic plague had killed more than 20 percent of the population of Europe. By the time it had run its course, four years after it arrived, 30 percent of the people were dead. Then the plague became dormant, or inactive, for a decade, only to resurface. Until well into the 1400s, the Black Death reappeared about every ten years, changing the Western world forever. After that, outbreaks of the plague happened less frequently and became more isolated.

As a result of the plague, entire cultures had to be rebuilt. The feudal system—in which wealthy landowners lived off the labor of their vassals, or serfs—began to crumble. On the other hand, land that had been too heavily farmed benefited from the chance to lie fallow and become fertile again. New trees grew in forests that had been depleted. The cultural reawakening known as the Renaissance brought new ideas to the world.

In 1665 the bubonic plague returned with a vengeance, surfacing in London, England. The nobility and other citizens who could fled to the countryside. Businesses shut down. "Dead carts" rumbled through the streets pushed by unemployed servants of the wealthy, crying out the somber message, "Bring out your dead!" The lord mayor of London, believing that the plague was spread by domestic animals, ordered the

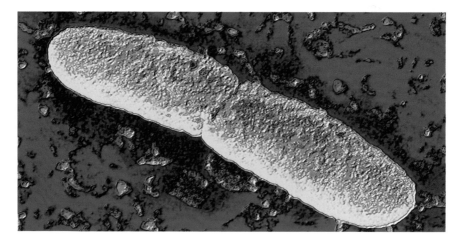

The bacterium that causes bubonic plague, Yersinia pestis, *shown magnified to twelve thousand times its actual size*

eradication of all dogs and cats. Quickly forty thousand dogs and two hundred thousand cats were killed. Without their natural enemy, the plague-carrying rats thrived, causing the plague to worsen. One hundred thousand Londoners died.

Just when it seemed that nothing could be worse, a fire started in a baker's shop and quickly set the city ablaze. For five days, the fire raged. When it was over, the heart of London was reduced to ashes. But this tragedy had a bright side. The fire also destroyed the nests of the rats that carried the plague. After the Great Fire of London, the plague ended.

Soon afterward, the bubonic plague disappeared from most of Europe, although it continued to devastate some areas of Russia, Egypt, and Asia during the next three hundred years.

In Europe the effective enforcement of quarantines, better housing, and better sanitation helped stop the plague. Some historians suggest that the increased population of gray rats, which do not carry the plague bacteria, helped reduce its spread.

The plague is still around. From time to time, a case appears, but bubonic plague is no longer a major epidemic in developed countries. Correctly diagnosed, it can be treated with an antibiotic drug. The spread of the disease can be prevented by rodent control and good hygiene practices.

(SMALLPOX)

Over the centuries, smallpox epidemics have also ravaged many countries around the world. Smallpox is caused by a virus that spreads from person to person, by touch or through breathing or coughing. The earliest recorded case of smallpox occurred in 1157 B.C., when an Egyptian pharaoh (ruler) named Ramses V was believed to have died of the disease.

Different strains of the virus produced different responses. Some cases were mild, while others were as deadly as the Black Death. The worst form of smallpox caused intense pain, high fever, and chills. Victims broke out in red, pus-filled sores, and their hands and feet swelled up. Skin fell away in strips, leaving the foul smell of rotting flesh. Large sores on victims' faces and backs bled, and their internal organs were damaged. Victims who did not die of smallpox were often sick for more than a month. They were left with deep scars called pockmarks on their skin. Many victims lost their sight. But those who recovered were immune to, or protected against, smallpox forever.

Smallpox epidemics erupted in Asia, India, and Europe throughout the Middle Ages and into the early 1800s. Because people who survived smallpox were immune afterward, there were lulls between epidemics. Then a new generation of children who were not immune to the disease would fall prey. In 1438, when smallpox swept through Paris, France, fifty thousand people died—most of whom were children under the age of twelve.

The most devastating impact of smallpox came with the European invasion of the Americas. When the Spanish conquistadors (conquerors) arrived in Central America in the early 1500s, they carried with them the smallpox virus, to which the indigenous (local) peoples had never been exposed. Because they had no immunity, the death toll was disastrous. In 1521 the disease spread through Tenochtitlán, the Aztec capital of Mexico. Spanish soldiers, led by Hernán Cortés, easily defeated the superior forces of the Aztec army because the Aztec warriors were dying of smallpox.

Throughout Mexico and Central America, village after village was destroyed by smallpox. Bodies lay in the fields and piled up in houses. The same thing happened in Brazil when

Portuguese colonists brought smallpox to South America.

In the early 1600s, British, French, and Dutch colonists arrived in North America. They, too, brought smallpox. The epidemic began in the Northeast and spread across the continent. Increase Mather, a Puritan leader, argued that God was clearly British, because the Indians died while the colonists did not. But Mather knew nothing about immunity.

In 1796 a British doctor named Edward Jenner observed that people who worked with cows often got a mild disease called cowpox. These people were not affected by smallpox—they were immune to it. He guessed that cowpox was a close cousin of smallpox and that a person who received a small dose of cowpox would be protected from smallpox. He tried a risky experiment—one that would be considered highly unethical in modern times—to test his idea. He stuck a needle into the pus of a cowpox sore and then scratched the cowpox fluid into the skin of a healthy young boy, James Phipps. Several weeks later, Dr. Jenner injected Phipps with the watery pus from a smallpox sore. Phipps did not catch smallpox. He was immune. Jenner called the procedure vaccinia, from *vacca*, the Latin word for "cow." These vaccinations, or inoculations, with cowpox gave people immunity to smallpox. The battle against smallpox had begun.

The principle of immunity is the basis for all vaccinations. The human immune system uses proteins called antibodies. When these proteins meet an invading germ, they attack it.

After the first attack, the body stores information about that invader, and if the same kind of microbe invades the body a second time, the antibodies will attack and destroy the invader immediately—before it can reproduce and cause a disease. If you receive a vaccination for mumps, you are given a very small dose of the mumps virus. Your body's antibodies destroy the

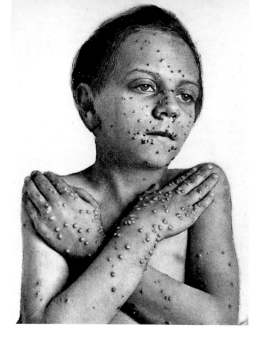

In 1915 this young boy suffered from the devastating effects of smallpox, including the characteristic sores.

virus. Your body will then remember the mumps virus, and if it ever invades again, the newly programmed antibodies will attack and destroy it before you even know you've been invaded. There are two types of vaccines. Some use live attenuated, or weakened, virus (mumps, measles, rubella) and others use inactivated, or killed, virus (influenza, hepatitis A and B). Sometimes vaccinations cause side effects or an allergic reaction. When you receive a vaccination, you will probably be warned about possible side effects, such as a slight fever or tenderness where you were vaccinated.

By the early 1900s, many countries had completely eliminated smallpox by enforced use of vaccines. In 1958, at a meeting of the World Health Organization, representatives of the Soviet Union (a union of fifteen republics that included Russia) suggested that WHO should organize a worldwide, cooperative effort to eradicate, or wipe out, smallpox.

A program to accomplish this seemingly overwhelming task was developed by Donald Henderson, a doctor from the United

States. In 1967 he assembled a team and began the task of eradicating smallpox where it still existed. Under his plan, when an outbreak of smallpox was reported, doctors from WHO would travel to the site. There, they would verify that the disease was indeed smallpox, quarantine the area, and vaccinate all quarantined individuals to prevent new cases of the disease.

Once organized, the effort required the services of thousands of workers around the world and cost more than $300 million. Most of the doctors and scientists who undertook this heroic and often dangerous task were young people fresh out of medical school. In November 1975, Dr. Henderson reported that what was believed to be the last case of smallpox had been found in a little girl in Bangladesh. She survived the disease.

But the battle was not quite over. In February 1977, soon after Dr. Henderson retired, smallpox appeared in the African nation of Somalia. This created a major problem. The area was in the middle of a war with the neighboring nation of Ethiopia. Refugees were fleeing the city of Ogaden, which was claimed by both Somalian and Ethiopian forces. Henderson's replacement on the smallpox project was a Japanese doctor named Isao Arita. Dr. Arita knew that by the end of the year, thousands of Somalian Muslims would celebrate a religious observance called the hajj by making a pilgrimage to Mecca, Saudi Arabia. In Mecca more than two million worshippers would gather. If just a few people infected with smallpox mingled in that crowd, all efforts to eliminate the disease would be lost for at least another decade—maybe forever.

Dr. Arita was determined. His teams pressed forward in search of smallpox victims, trying to beat the hajj deadline. The war continued. The rainy season came, and mudflows blocked roads. But the doctors did not give up. They drove through

In the late 1970s, posters all over the streets of Mogadishu, Somalia, offered a reward equal to thirty-three dollars to anyone who reported a smallpox case.

the rain and the muck. They asked questions and examined sick people. They vaccinated everyone they could find.

Finally, in the town of Merka, Somalia, they found a lean, wiry man named Ali Maow Maalin, who had the last known case of smallpox. They watched and waited. Maalin recovered and became immune. WHO doctors waited some more. No one else in Maalin's family or town or anywhere in Somalia came down with smallpox.

On May 8, 1980, WHO declared victory over smallpox. All traces of the disease had been eliminated. The only remaining samples of the virus were frozen in secure vaults at the CDC in Atlanta, Georgia, and at a similar center in Koltsovo, Russia.

An advisory committee to the WHO recommended the total destruction of both the U.S. and Russian specimens so that no trace of the deadly virus would exist in the world. When all parties had agreed and the disposal date had been set, the U.S. representatives learned that the Russian repositories of the smallpox specimens had not been entirely secure. Secretly, the Russians had stockpiled some of the smallpox vaccine. As a result, the frozen vials were not destroyed. In the twenty-first century, these vials are essential as a "starter virus" for research exploring the structure of this deadly virus, particularly in light of the potential for a smallpox bioterrorist attack. Without this, Americans would be defenseless against a potential smallpox bioterrorist attack. The vials are preserved in the vaults at the CDC in Atlanta and presumably also in Russia.

(ANTHRAX)

Anthrax is primarily a disease of herbivorous (plant-eating) animals such as cattle and sheep. Transmission to humans is usually related to those who farm the animals or work in the textile industry. Through history, anthrax has been known by a number of different names including woolsorters' disease, ragpickers' disease, and the Siberian plague.

Since antiquity, anthrax has existed in many parts of the world. The fifth of the ten plagues reported in the Old Testament of the Bible, in which all of Egypt's cattle died, may have been anthrax, according to Chester Drum, an anthrax researcher at the University of Chicago in Illinois. The sixth plague, the plague of boils, may also have been anthrax, this time affecting humans. The worst anthrax outbreak in history was probably the Black Bane, an epidemic that spread through Europe in the 1600s. It resulted in the deaths of many thousands of humans and animals.

The disease is devastating to farm animals. Horses, oxen, cows, sheep, and goats stricken by anthrax fall behind the herd. An infected animal's head lowers, its breathing becomes heavy, and it quickly falls dead, often with its belly grotesquely swollen.

The progress of the disease is so fast that herders and farmers can only watch helplessly as their animals die.

Until the end of the nineteenth century, people were at a loss to understand the cause of this terrible pestilence. Blame was placed on stagnant water, insects, overexposure to hot sun, deadly gases from marshes, or poisoned weeds. Some pastures were thought to have been cursed by sorcerers, because animals who grazed in these places died of anthrax.

In 1876 physician Robert Koch demonstrated that a rod-shaped bacterium, *Bacillus anthracis*, causes anthrax. Through his studies of *Bacillus anthracis*, Koch developed a series of steps that are still used to determine whether a particular bacterium causes a specific disease. These steps are called Koch's postulates.

In 1877 herds in central France were particularly hard hit by recurring outbreaks of anthrax. The French minister of agriculture called for help from Louis Pasteur, who had earlier in that century established that bacteria cause diseases. Pasteur knew that anthrax was caused by a bacterium, but fashioning a vaccine proved to be difficult. On August 18, 1878, he opened a laboratory near Chartres, France, with collaborators Charles Chamberland, August Vinsot, and Emile Roux. By 1881 they had developed a vaccine to protect the herds.

Bacillus anthracis lives naturally in certain types of soils. Hardy forms of the bacterium, called spores, can survive for years in soil or on contaminated objects. Animals are infected when they ingest spores while grazing, breathe in spores, or eat animals that died of anthrax. Once inside a host, the bacteria enter the blood or tissues, where they multiply and release deadly toxins that cause the symptoms of the disease.

The occurrence of anthrax in humans has, historically, been limited. People generally are infected due to contact with infected animals or animal products such as wool or hides. In countries with effective public health programs, such as the United States, human infection is rare. The disease has become important as a threat to humans in the United States only because of its potential as a weapon of bioterrorism.

In people, anthrax occurs in three forms: cutaneous (affecting the skin), intestinal (intestines), and inhalation (lungs). At least 95 percent of all cases of anthrax are the cutaneous form.

Cutaneous anthrax occurs when bacteria enter the body through a break in the skin. The disease begins as an itchy bump that develops into a painless ulcer with a black center. Cutaneous anthrax is easily diagnosed and cured.

Intestinal anthrax results from eating undercooked meat from anthrax-infected animals. It is seldom seen in the United States because of thorough inspection of livestock. The symptoms include nausea, loss of appetite, vomiting, and fever, followed by abdominal pain, vomiting of blood, and severe diarrhea. Without treatment, the disease can be fatal.

Inhalation anthrax, caused by breathing in anthrax spores, is rare. This form is the most dangerous. From the lungs, spores quickly reach the bloodstream, where they multiply rapidly. The disease progresses swiftly, so early diagnosis and treatment are critical. Early symptoms resemble those of flu, with sudden fever, difficulty breathing, and sweating. In the final stages, the patient develops severe breathing problems and goes into shock. The skin turns bluish. Death can follow in just a few hours.

Early treatment of anthrax is important, but diagnosis of the inhalation and intestinal forms can be difficult. Anthrax is diagnosed by isolating *Bacillus anthracis* from the blood, skin ulcers, or lung secretions, or by measuring specific antibodies in the blood. The disease is treated with antibiotics.

CHAPTER FOUR

From the Tropics to the Tundra:
Malaria, Influenza, and Diphtheria

Major infectious diseases have continued to ravage communities and countries into modern times. Vaccines, antibiotics, and other medicines have helped reduce the danger, but infectious diseases still challenge physicians' and scientists' skills and knowledge. Malaria, influenza, and diphtheria are diseases that have pushed people to dramatic feats.

(A DEADLY MOSQUITO BITE)

Malaria is a disease that occurs in tropical and subtropical regions of the world. It is spread by the bite of female mosquitoes—not just any mosquito but certain species of *Anopheles* mosquitoes. Malaria is not the only disease borne by mosquitoes. Yellow fever, dengue fever, West Nile virus, and encephalitis are other major diseases carried by mosquitoes.

Malaria transmission happens in three basic stages. First, a female mosquito bites a human, sucking in the person's blood. If the human has malaria, then his or her blood contains *Plasmodium* parasites—the cause of malaria. These parasites enter

Doctors, army officers, and reporters donned surgical gowns and masks in a 1918 tour of hospitals to observe the treatment of Spanish flu patients.

the mosquito with the person's blood and flow to the mosquito's stomach, where they reproduce. When the mosquito bites another human, the parasites are transferred into the human's blood. In the person's bloodstream, the parasites are carried into the liver, where they reproduce and invade red blood cells. Eventually the parasites cause the red blood cells to burst, sending more parasites into the bloodstream to start the cycle again. During these periods when parasites flood the bloodstream, the person has bouts of fever and may die.

Over the centuries, malaria has sickened and killed millions of people. Malaria causes fever, chills, nausea, muscle and joint pain, weakness, vomiting, and sometimes convulsions or coma. In the United States, malaria was a serious problem until the mid-1930s. By 1950, thanks to effective mosquito control, improved medicines, and a higher standard of living, the disease had been almost completely eliminated in the United States. Malaria is still widespread in Central and South America, Africa, Southeast Asia, India, and Indonesia.

In the past, many people believed that malaria was caused by bad air—the word *malaria* means "bad air" in Italian. They thought that unhealthy vapors, or miasmas, came from swamps, low-lying lands, and bogs. Although some cultures in East Africa had long attributed malaria to mosquito bites, most European scientists and physicians dismissed this notion as folklore.

In 1807 Dr. John Crawford of Baltimore, Maryland, was ridiculed for publishing a paper that suggested malaria could be transmitted when mosquitoes laid their eggs in humans. Ninety years later, he was proved to be closer to the truth than those who had laughed at his idea.

In 1884 a French army doctor named Charles Laveran, who was serving in Algeria in Africa, began examining droplets of

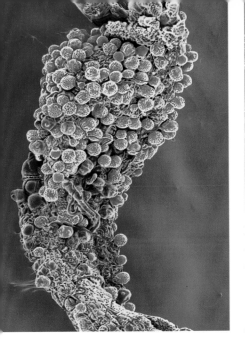

Left: *A false-color scanning electron micrograph of the stomach wall of a mosquito infected with malarial parasites (the round blue objects). The parasites are in an early stage in their life cycle.*

Above: *A female Anopheles mosquito*

blood taken from French soldiers who had malaria. He noticed that malaria patients' blood contained more red blood cells than healthy blood contained. He was even more mystified by something that happened as he watched the blood under the glass of his microscope. Sometimes the red blood cells would expand and swell and finally burst open, releasing malaria-causing parasites. But many scientists of the time doubted the validity of Dr. Laveran's discovery.

At about the same time, Dr. Patrick Manson, a British physician working in India, developed the hypothesis that mosquitoes were the likely carriers of malaria. This hypothesis was an inspired guess that Dr. Manson arrived at by looking for a common association between the disease and the environment. He observed that malaria appeared in areas with a warm climate and swampy lands. In these areas, the most common insect was the mosquito, which bites humans.

This was a good start, but not a definite link. Later, a British scientist-poet, Ronald Ross, put the theories of Dr. Laveran and Dr. Manson to a scientific test. Ross had invented a portable microscope, which he carried with him on his assignment to a British regiment in India. There, he began a painstaking quest to isolate in mosquitoes the same parasite that Dr. Laveran had seen in malaria patients' blood. He corresponded with Dr. Manson and studied the work of Dr. Laveran as he pursued his investigation.

Ross collected mosquitoes and persuaded "volunteers" who had malaria to let these mosquitoes bite them. Using pins for tools, Ross dissected the mosquitoes and examined them under his portable microscope, looking for the *Plasmodium* parasites. For two years, Ross pursued his research without success. The problem was that he was looking at the wrong mosquitoes. He did not know that only certain kinds of mosquitoes carry malaria.

In Sigur Ghat, a valley in India where coffee plantations thrived, Ross finally found his answer. There he identified *Anopheles* mosquitoes. When he examined these insects, he found plasmodia. In 1898 he observed that the *Plasmodium* parasites reproduced in the mosquito's stomach and then entered the saliva. This was the way the parasite traveled from mosquito to human.

(CONTROLLING MALARIA)

In 1881 a French company launched an effort to build a canal that would connect the Atlantic Ocean with the Pacific Ocean across the narrow Isthmus of Panama. The company was defeated, not by the enormity of the task but by malaria-carrying mosquitoes. One writer reported that because of the mosquitoes, only 20 percent of the workers who came to Panama remained for more than two months, and those who did stay were often so weakened by malaria that they could not work.

A worker applies poison in an attempt to control the spread of mosquitoes during the construction of the Panama Canal in the early 1900s.

After eight years of attempts and failure, the French company gave up, and the United States bought the rights to build the canal. President Theodore Roosevelt assigned Colonel William C. Gorgas, an army doctor, the task of destroying the mosquitoes that caused malaria and yellow fever.

For two years, Colonel Gorgas commanded his forces to drain swamps and dry up places where water might collect. The soldiers also cleared weeds and covered mosquito breeding areas with a solution of carbolic acid, resin, and caustic soda. Their mission was to eliminate any area where mosquitoes could breed. They also built screens around the shacks where workers lived, and Colonel Gorgas hired additional laborers for ten cents an hour to stay in the living quarters and swat or capture mosquitoes. Gorgas's campaign succeeded in reducing the mosquito population. In turn, the incidence of yellow fever and malaria dropped, and the Panama Canal was completed in 1914.

Twenty-seven years later, after Japanese forces bombed Pearl Harbor, Hawaii, in 1941, U.S. military leaders saw a need to establish year-round training bases in southern states for the

U.S. armed forces. To do this, they had to deal with malaria, which was still a problem in the South. The surgeon general of the United States, Thomas Parran, created the National Defense Malaria Control Activities office to tackle the issue. The

YELLOW FEVER AND THE LOUISIANA PURCHASE

Another disease carried by mosquitoes is yellow fever. The virus that causes yellow fever is carried by female *Aedes aegypti* mosquitoes, which get the virus from monkeys. The virus lives in monkeys without causing illness. When an infected mosquito bites a human, the virus passes with the mosquito's saliva into the person's bloodstream.

A. aegypti mosquitoes prefer to lay their eggs in containers of clean water. They often lay eggs in cups and pots where rainwater collects. These mosquitoes are as likely to breed in cities and towns as in swamps.

Yellow fever may have spread to the Americas by mosquitoes breeding in the ships sailing with Columbus in 1492. The disease wiped out entire populations in the Caribbean, paving the way for European conquests.

In 1802 Napoléon Bonaparte, the emperor of France, sent 33,000 soldiers to French-ruled Haiti, located on an island in the Caribbean Sea, to stop a revolt by slaves led by Toussaint Louverture. But yellow fever struck down more than 85 percent of Napoléon's army. This left the Haitians, most of whom were immune to yellow fever, to control their own nation.

The devastation wrought by yellow fever undoubtedly helped persuade Napoléon that land in the New World was not worth the taking. Consequently, in 1803 he was ready to deal with U.S. president Thomas Jefferson and sell the Louisiana Territory to the United States in a deal known as the Louisiana Purchase.

office was headquartered in Atlanta, Georgia, because the large Okefenokee swamp in southeastern Georgia provided an ideal breeding ground for mosquitoes.

The malaria office opened on Peachtree Street in Atlanta. Very quickly, more than four thousand mosquito warriors began spraying DDT pesticide, Paris Green, and diesel oil on every suspected breeding place. They covered Puerto Rico, the Virgin Islands, and the southern United States from Florida to California. This concentrated effort virtually eliminated malaria in the United States. But the malaria office did not close its doors—it began to deal with other diseases and ultimately became the Centers for Disease Control and Prevention.

(TREATING MALARIA)

For centuries the only known treatment for malaria was quinine. Quinine contains a compound called quinoline, which is found in the bark of the cinchona tree. Quinoline kills the *Plasmodium* parasite. In the early 1600s, Jesuit missionaries (religious workers) traveling in South America learned of the curative powers of the bark of the cinchona tree and brought it to Europe.

Two hundred years later, Charles Ledger, an British adventurer, wandered through the mountains and forests of Peru, looking for valuable quinine-producing cinchona trees. He succeeded, and he gathered seeds from the trees to take back to Great Britain. He believed that with these seeds, he would become honored and wealthy. But the British government did not recognize the value of his find. Ledger was disappointed but determined. He approached several governments in Europe, offering to sell the seeds of trees that had the power to cure malaria. He finally found a country that was interested. The Dutch government appreciated the importance of the cinchona tree and the value of the seeds. Dutch officials purchased Ledger's seeds and began planting cinchona plantations on the island of Java, a Dutch colony in Indonesia. Ledger received a salary for life, and the scientific name of the cinchona tree— *Cinchona ledgeriana*—bears his name.

Until World War II (1939–1945), the Dutch government maintained a monopoly on naturally grown quinine. During this war, however, the Japanese military gained control of the cinchona plantations in the Dutch East Indies (Indonesia), hoping that this move would cripple U.S. forces. These islands provided the principal source for quinine, since the cinchona trees in South America had died in the mid-1800s. The Japanese reasoned that the Americans could not do battle in the mosquito-infested islands of the South Pacific without quinine for the soldiers.

More than five hundred thousand U.S. soldiers did suffer from malaria during the battles in the South Pacific. But the widespread use of DDT to kill mosquitoes and the development of quinacrine, a synthetic substitute for quinine, took away the Japanese army's advantage.

Several modern medicines, including chloroquine, mefloquine, atovaquone-proguanil, and primaquine, have been able to cure most cases of malaria. Mosquito control also reduces malaria outbreaks. But the war against malaria is far from won. Emerging parasites have become resistant to almost all classes of antimalarial drugs. Some new breeds of mosquitoes are resistant to DDT and other insecticides. A second battle against malaria has begun.

Although malaria is no longer a threatening disease in the

United States, it is still a major threat in many places in the world. Forty percent of the world's people live in regions where malaria is a problem. It is estimated that more than 350 million new cases of malaria occur worldwide each year, and between 1 and 2 million people die each year of the disease.

(THE SPANISH FLU EPIDEMIC)

Every fall, state health departments make announcements about that season's flu shot. If you wonder why you may need a new flu shot each year, it's because influenza—the flu—is caused by a virus that is very unstable. It changes into new strains all the time. The flu virus is a sphere with little peaks, or spikes, sticking out. Each year, new strains of flu emerge, and each strain (usually named for the place it was first detected) is slightly different. Because of the continuous changes, any particular flu vaccine will not be effective against another strain of flu.

The worst epidemic ever to strike the United States was the influenza outbreak of 1918, called the Spanish flu. It swept across the United States and around the world, becoming a pandemic. Normally, influenza is not deadly to healthy young people, although it can be fatal to older people or people who suffer other serious ailments. But the Spanish flu swiftly killed healthy young men and women.

It first appeared on March 11, 1918, at Fort Riley, Kansas, where nearly one hundred soldiers suddenly became ill on the same day. From Kansas the virus traveled with the soldiers overseas to the battlefields of Europe, where World War I (1914–1918) was being fought. The virus passed from man to man in wet, muddy trenches, in the crowded barracks, and on troop ships.

Some soldiers died from this terrible flu. Others brought it back to their home countries, traveling by ship or train across the world.

German soldiers called the flu the Blitz Katarrh, while British soldiers called it Flanders grippe. U.S. soldiers, mistakenly believing that the illness had come from Spain, called it Spanish flu or Spanish lady.

The Spanish flu reached around the world, from the tropics to the poles. More than twenty million people died, including more than five hundred thousand Americans. Ten times as many people died at home in the United States from the flu as died in combat in World War I. Many victims died of a bacterial pneumonia brought on by the flu, but most died of the flu itself.

Illness and death were everywhere. Businesses slowed down or stopped. Schools, movie theaters, and other public places were closed because so many people were sick. People wore face masks to halt the spread of the flu germ.

In San Francisco, California, public health officials passed an ordinance forbidding anyone from appearing in public without a face mask. At the University of Michigan at Ann Arbor, any student caught without a mask was automatically suspended. In some cities, streetcar conductors refused to allow passengers to ride without a face mask. A town in Arizona passed a law forbidding people from shaking hands.

The epidemic spread during the summer of 1918, reaching its peak in the fall. Then it waned, reappeared in 1919, and finally disappeared as mysteriously as it had begun. At the time of the epidemic, no one knew what was causing it. Researchers attempted to isolate and identify the microbe. It wasn't found until the mid-1930s, when Dr. Richard Shope found the biological mixture that had proved so destructive. He suggested that the flu was caused by a combination of a virus and a bacterium,

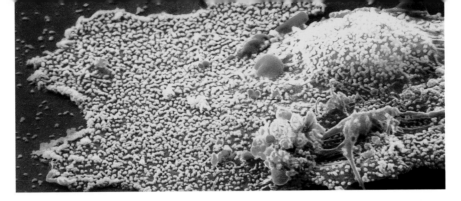

Influenza viruses (the tiny yellow spheres) have invaded this cell. Like other viruses, flu viruses take control of the cell and turn the nucleus (light red) into a factory for producing more viruses.

Pfeiffer's bacillus, found in pigs. Dr. Shope believed that when these microbes moved from pigs to humans, they caused a deadly combination of viral flu (called swine flu) and bacterial pneumonia. Some physicians haven't accepted this theory, however. Many microbes live only in certain animals and do not infect humans. Some of these microbes are harmless to the animal—they do not cause disease in the animal. Other microbes cause disease in animals, but not humans. But sometimes microbes mutate, and then they can jump from an animal to a human. To mutate means that some part of an organism's molecular structure changes. Viruses that do not change to meet new conditions will not survive, while viruses that do mutate may live.

When viruses or bacteria mutate, a disease that had previously affected only animals may move into a human host. This can happen when people live close to animals, as farmers do, or when humans invade a microbe's natural habitat such as by clearing jungles to build farms and towns. The Spanish flu epidemic was thought to be caused by a virus that had mutated and jumped from pigs to humans.

Fifty years later, few U.S. citizens remembered the horrors of the Spanish flu. But epidemiologists did remember. In January 1976, Dr. Martin Goldfield, the chief of epidemiology for the state of New Jersey, recognized a swine flu-type virus in blood taken from a soldier who had died from influenza at Fort Dix, New Jersey. Alarmed, Dr. Goldfield promptly sent samples to the CDC in Atlanta.

By the 1970s, doctors knew that the 1918 flu virus had jumped from pigs to humans and then spread from human to human. While a milder variety of swine flu had been known to infect farmers who raised hogs, this case of influenza—in a soldier who had had no contact with pigs—suggested human-to-human transmission.

At the urging of doctors at the CDC, the U.S. government initiated a massive drive to manufacture and distribute a vaccine to protect millions of citizens against swine flu in order to prevent an epidemic. More than 40 million shots were administered in October and November 1976. But this was the epidemic that never was. Wherever the virus had come from to kill the soldier at Fort Dix, it no longer seemed to exist. For almost a year, no more cases of swine flu appeared. But a new problem developed.

Cases of Guillain-Barré syndrome, a rare paralytic disease, began to occur a few weeks after the swine flu inoculation program began. Some physicians worried that the number of cases was high enough to raise the question of whether the disease had any relationship to the mass vaccination program administered during the fall of 1976. Flu vaccinations do carry a slight possibility of side effects, such as pain and swelling at the spot where the shot is injected, a slight fever, or a mild case of the flu. On rare occasions, a more serious reaction will occur.

The doctors needed a baseline, a measurement of the normal incidence of Guillain-Barré syndrome in the population over a given period of time. This would help them determine if the current number of cases was higher than usual. The doctors turned to the Mayo Clinic for help. Dr. Leonard Kurland, chief of epidemiology, had the answer. By looking at the normally occurring incidence of the disease, as measured by the clinic's extensive population records, Dr. Kurland could calculate whether there might have been an increase in Guillain-Barré following the vaccinations. The answer was yes.

The initial epidemiological information suggested that the occurrence of this disease had increased seven times. No one knew then or knows yet the actual cause of this form of paralysis. But health officials were disturbed by the new information. Health officials from around the country discussed the situation and decided to end the swine flu vaccination program immediately. Within ten weeks, the number of newly reported Guillain-Barré cases fell back to normal levels.

(A LIFE-OR-DEATH RACE IN ALASKA)

Diphtheria is a contagious disease that causes a victim's throat to swell, cutting off his or her breathing. In the United States, diphtheria is prevented by the DPT vaccination (a combination of diphtheria, pertussis-whooping cough, and tetanus vaccines), which is given to young children. The diphtheria bacterium, *Corynebacterium diphtheriae*, produces a powerful poison called an exotoxin. A patient who is infected with diphtheria must receive an antitoxin—a serum that blocks the action of the poison. It has become standard to follow this with antibiotics. Without the antitoxin, victims are doomed to slow, painful suffocation.

Before diphtheria vaccinations became available in 1923, epidemics of this "malignant throat distemper" often swept through communities in colonial America. Most victims were

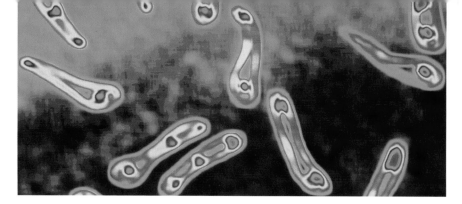

Corynebacterium diphtheriae, *the bacterium that causes diphtheria,*
produces a toxin, causing inflammation of the throat and tonsils and
damage to the heart and nervous system.

children. Many historians believe that the first president of the
United States, George Washington, died of diphtheria.

In 1925 the most dramatic diphtheria epidemic in U.S. history happened in Nome, Alaska, where the newly developed
vaccine had not yet been introduced. During an average winter
in Nome, temperatures often plunge to –20°F (–29°C). But in
January 1925, a cold wind blowing eastward from the Bering
Strait made the temperature drop even lower.

Nome was isolated from the rest of the world in the winter,
and Dr. Curtis Welch was the only doctor in this city of two
thousand citizens. On January 21, he was called to a home
to see a sick child. The child had a high fever and a very sore
throat. This was not unusual, but when Dr. Welch peered into
the child's throat, he saw that it had turned from healthy red
to white. A toxin was killing the cells lining the child's throat.
This was diphtheria!

Before the day was over, two more children came down with
the same symptoms. Dr. Welch immediately recognized the potential for a deadly epidemic. He had no antitoxin, and none of
the children in Nome had been vaccinated against diphtheria.

The doctor rushed to the telegraph office. The town's
telegraph operator hurriedly tapped Dr. Welch's frantic plea

to public health offices in Fairbanks and Anchorage, Alaskan towns that are thousands of miles away. He needed antitoxin, and he needed it right away.

Telegraph lines around the country buzzed. Dr. J. B. Beeson at the Alaska Railroad Hospital in Anchorage had the needed units of antitoxin serum. (Serum is a fluid containing the antitoxin.) The problem was, how would they get the serum to Nome? A railroad line ran north from Anchorage to Fairbanks, but the closest that it came to Nome was the station at Nenana, and that was still 675 miles (1,086 kilometers) away from Nome. No airplanes were available, and even if there were, the weather was turning bad. A winter storm was forming in the Bering Strait.

The governor of Alaska decided that the only reliable way to get the serum from Nenana to Nome was by dogsled, along the Iditarod Trail, one of several major winter routes. This trail, named for the town of Iditarod, was used primarily by dogsled mushers who carried supplies, mail, and a few passengers. By telegraph communication, relay teams of drivers and dogs were organized and assigned portions of the trail to cover.

Meanwhile, the first child died and two others lay dying. Other cases of diphtheria broke out. Normally, the trip from Nenana to Nome took twenty days by dogsled. If this trip took that long, however, the serum would be too late.

Dr. Beeson carefully bottled the serum, wrapped it, and packed it. The 20-pound (9 kg) package was loaded on the train in Anchorage, and the train headed north to Nenana. At eleven on the night of January 27, the train steamed into Nenana. The package was handed to William "Wild Bill" Shannon, who set out immediately into the dark of a long Alaskan winter night with ten powerful husky dogs pulling his sled. The temperature had dropped to –30°F (–34°C), and the wind was rising.

While telegraph reports flashed the news to newspapers all around the United States, the race against the deadly diphtheria bacteria began. About twenty men and their dogs headed toward their assigned places along the trail. The men, sleds, and dogs carried the serum across the vast, snow-covered land, over the Yukon River, and steadily westward toward Nome. At each stop—including Tolovana, Tanana, Nine Mile, Ruby, Whiskey Creek, Galena, Bishop Mountain, Old Woman, and Unalakleet—the next man was ready to take over his leg of the journey.

Charlie Evans was miles short of his destination of Nulato when his two lead sled dogs fell over dead. But Evans did not quit. He hooked the dogs' harnesses to himself and led his dogs onward, racing into the howling wind and bitter cold. The temperature was so cold that if a man lost his gloves, his hands would freeze in minutes.

Meanwhile, Leonhard Seppala, a renowned dog-racing champion who lived in Nome, hitched his dogs behind his lead dog, Togo, and headed east to meet the approaching dog teams. After traveling over 160 miles (259 km), with one stop at a friend's igloo, he picked up the serum at Shaktoolik and headed back toward Nome. The day before, he had made a dangerous crossing on the ice of Norton Bay. This direct route had saved 100 miles (162 km) of travel. Now he needed to recross the bay in a fierce wind. He knew that if the wind shifted, the ice could be blown out of the bay, carrying him, his dogs, his sled, and the serum out to sea. But time was running out for the children of Nome. Seppala did not hesitate. About 86 miles (139 km) later, he reached the western shore of Norton Bay, just as the wind began pushing the ice pack out of the bay. Seppala stopped at a roadhouse in Golovin, where he collapsed for needed warmth, food, and rest. Charlie Olson took the serum and headed west.

The next 25 miles (40 km) along the trail were the most difficult. The wind was now slicing directly across the trail, throwing the driver, sled, and dogs off the trail repeatedly. Olson pushed forward. He suffered severe frostbite, but he made it to the Bluff roadhouse, where he met the next driver, Gunnar Kaasen.

The blizzard was intensifying. Kaasen was 53 miles (86 km) from Nome, and Ed Rohn was racing to meet him for the final leg. In the blindness of the blizzard, however, the men did not meet, and Kaasen had no choice but to keep going. Suddenly, a powerful gust of wind blew his sled onto its side, tossing the package of serum into the snow. Frantically, Kaasen sifted through the whirling, twisting snow. Miraculously, he found the package.

He rushed on through the night, led by his lead husky, Balto. Totally blinded by the snow, Kaasen half rode and half ran as the powerful dogs pressed forward into the blizzard. Suddenly, the sound of the wind changed pitch. The wail of the wind softened. They were between the buildings of Nome. They had made it!

Inside the hospital, Dr. Welch heard a dog bark. He eased open the front door, which caught in the wind and jerked him out into the storm. There stood Gunnar Kaasen, his smile almost hidden beneath his fur hat and his beard layered with frost and snow. Kaasen held up both hands, cradling the precious cargo. The relay team had reached Nome in a record-setting five days and seven hours. By then five children had died, but another twenty-nine were saved from terrible strangulation by diphtheria.

This amazing rescue is remembered each year during the annual Iditarod dogsled race in Alaska. And in Central Park, in the middle of Manhattan in New York City, a large bronze statue of an Alaskan husky named Balto honors the twenty drivers and 150 dogs who carried antitoxin serum to Nome in the winter of 1925.

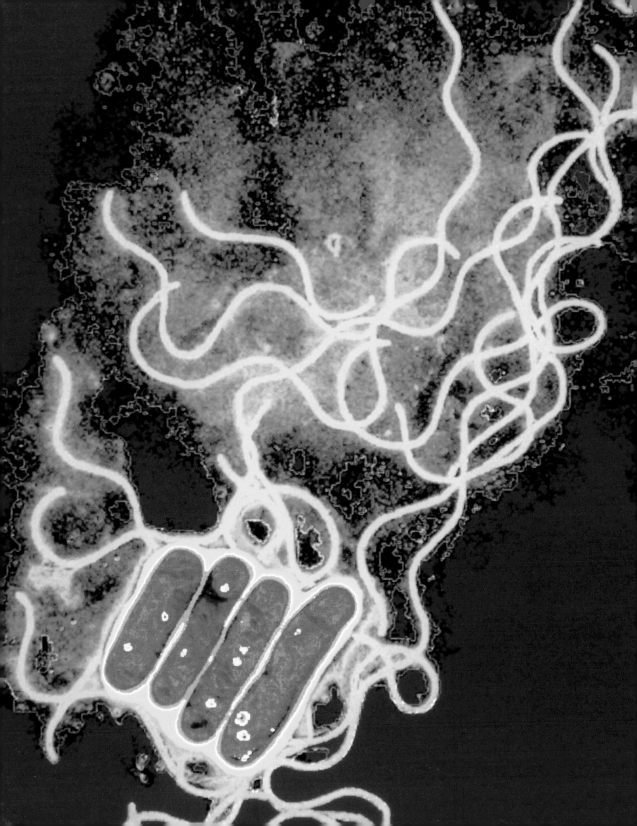

CHAPTER FIVE

Modern Killers:
Legionnaires' Disease, Ebola, and Muerto Canyon Virus

In 1928, thanks to a serendipitous accident, a powerful new weapon was developed to help fight bacterial diseases. That year a Scottish scientist named Alexander Fleming went off for a week on a vacation. Before he left, he had been growing a common type of bacteria, staphylococcus (or, staph), in his laboratory. While he was gone, a mold (a form of fungus) floated through the air in the lab. A fleck of that mold landed in Fleming's culture of staph bacteria. Amazingly, where the mold landed, the bacteria died.

When Fleming returned from vacation and saw that the staphylococci had died near the mold, he immediately realized the significance of the observation. He used the mold, *Penicillium*, as the basis to create the "miracle drug" penicillin, which worked to stop many bacterial diseases.

Since then antibiotics such as penicillin have been effective in fighting a wide range of bacterial diseases. Many people thought that with antibiotic drugs, humans had won the war against microbes. But that dream has been shattered as new epidemics have continued to arise with deadly force.

Legionnella pneumophila *bacteria cause the deadly Legionnaires' disease.*

(EPIDEMIC IN PHILADELPHIA)

During the summer of 1976, while much of the United States celebrated the nation's bicentennial, medical experts debated whether the Spanish flu epidemic of 1918 would resurface as a swine flu epidemic that winter. That summer in Philadelphia, Pennsylvania, where the Declaration of Independence had been signed two hundred years earlier, members of the American Legion, the country's largest veterans' organization, attended a convention. Hundreds of Legionnaires and their wives attended meetings and banquets and partied at four hotels in the City of Brotherly Love.

It was mid-July and hot. Suddenly, two men fell ill with high fever, aching muscles, and pneumonia. These cases were followed by many more. All the victims were men and women who had attended the Legionnaires' convention. By August 2, 8 people were dead and 150 were ill. Before it was over, 29 people had died from the swiftly striking acute form of pneumonia.

Was it the dreaded swine flu? With all the attention that had been given to the threat of an epidemic, many people believed the flu had struck again.

Doctors rushed tissue and blood samples from the patients to the CDC. Within a day, the scientists had ruled out influenza viruses as the cause. It was not swine flu. Labeled by the media as "Legionnaire killer" and "killer pneumonia," the outbreak caused public panic. What was this epidemic?

Dr. David Fraser, an experienced epidemiologist, was sent from Atlanta to lead the investigation. His team questioned hundreds of Legionnaires and their families. The medical detectives were looking for the one thing all these people had in common. They knew that all the victims had attended the convention, but that was not enough. Many people who had

An outbreak of Legionnaires' disease occurred at the Bellevue Stratford Hotel in Philadelphia in July 1976.

attended had not gotten sick. The epidemiologists asked detailed questions. Who got the disease—old or young people, men or women? When did they arrive? How did they travel?

What, when, and where did they eat? Where did they go while they were in Philadelphia? Where did they stay?

The detective work paid off. The epidemiologists analyzed their data to find the common denominator among those who had fallen ill. Although all the Legionnaires had attended the convention, they had not all stayed at the same hotel. The one thing those who became ill had in common was that they had all stayed at the Bellevue Stratford Hotel, a famous old hotel in the heart of Philadelphia.

With that important fact determined, the search began for a microbe or toxic chemical that could have caused the outbreak. Back in Atlanta, microbiologist Dr. Joseph McDade and physician-scientist Dr. Charles "Shep" Shepard tried every test they could think of on the blood samples from people who had gotten the disease. But they couldn't find a chemical or microbe that would account for the symptoms. Although the scientists suspected that a microbe rather than a chemical had caused the outbreak, they could not isolate a bacterium or virus in the blood samples. No microbes showed up in the ordinary culture. The doctors tried different nutrients as a culture. Finally, when they used untreated eggs as a culture, they succeeded. A new bacterium grew this time.

By January 1977, the CDC epidemiologists had found the culprit—a bacterium they called *Legionella pneumophila*. They also made another discovery. When they examined blood samples from several previous unsolved cases of disease—outbreaks of pneumonia in Washington, D.C., in 1965, and in Pontiac, Michigan, in 1968—these samples contained *Legionella* bacteria. *Legionella* bacteria normally lie dormant in puddles of water. Air-conditioning towers, such as the one at the Bellevue Stratford, provide a perfect breeding ground for them. The bacteria had traveled in airborne water droplets through the hotel's air-conditioning ducts to find warm hosts in the guests and hotel workers who breathed in the microbes.

Since then smaller outbreaks of Legionnaires' disease have been reported, and *Legionella* bacteria have been found in showerheads and water faucet pipes. Hot tubs, humidifiers, and decorative fountains can also harbor these and other bacteria. Fortunately, Legionnaires' disease cannot spread from person to person.

(A DEADLY VIRUS FROM THE RAIN FOREST)

In September 1976, not long after the Legionnaires fell sick in Philadelphia, an outbreak occurred on the other side of the world. In northern Zaire (since renamed the Democratic Republic of Congo), a country in central Africa, a young man received an injection of medicine at the small Yambuku Mission Hospital. The village of Yambuku is in the Bumba Zone, an area of rain forests near the Ebola River. Local people suffering from malaria would come to the hospital in Yambuku to get shots of medicine to ease their chills and pains. Because the hospital staff had little money to buy supplies, they used the same few unsterilized needles to inject hundreds of patients.

A couple of days after the young man, who taught at the local school, received his injection, he became ill again. First, he had a headache. Then he began to sweat from a fever, and the joints of his arms and legs ached. As the days passed, he rapidly grew sicker. A rash appeared on his face and then all over his body. He began to shake and tremble. The red spots on his body turned to large blotches and then bruises. The teacher's skin became soft and pulpy, and chunks of it fell off his body. Blood oozed from his mouth, and he vomited a black, slippery substance. His insides were being turned into a slimy jelly. Blood flowed from his eyes as he went into a seizure. His body twitched, and his arms and legs thrashed. After three days, he died. He was the first victim of one of the deadliest diseases in the world—Ebola hemorrhagic fever.

Shortly after the teacher's death, thirteen of the seventeen staff workers at the hospital died in the same way. One of the nuns who had treated the teacher flew to Kinshasa, the capital of Zaire, to seek a cure. But the doctors at Ngaliema Hospital in Kinshasa could not help her, and she also died.

The young nurse at the hospital who had been caring for the nun when the nun died was named Mayinga. She tried to protect herself from the disease by wearing gloves and a face mask, but she could not avoid contact with the nun's blood. Soon Mayinga, too, began to feel ill. But she ignored her illness and went to take care of some business at a government office, where she stood in line with hundreds of people. While waiting, she shared a bottled soft drink with a stranger. The next day, Mayinga was feeling worse. She went to Kinshasa's largest hospital, the Mama Yemo Hospital. The doctors told her she was not very sick and sent her back to Ngaliema Hospital. At the same time, rumors began to circulate throughout the city about a deadly new disease coming out of the Bumba Zone.

When people at Ngaliema Hospital realized that Mayinga had this new disease, they panicked. They alerted government officials, who became immediately alarmed. Kinshasa is a large city, whose population at that time numbered more than two million people, with direct links by air to other cities around the world. This disease was fatal, contagious—and without a cure. It would be a disaster if it spread.

Mobutu Sese Seko, who was then president of Zaire, sent in his army to seal off the infected areas. Soldiers surrounded the Ngaliema Hospital. No one could enter or leave. All roads in the Bumba Zone were blocked. No one was allowed in or out. The World Health Organization was also alerted.

The first photograph of the Zaire strain of the Ebola virus was taken in 1976 by Dr. F. A. Murphy at the CDC.

The doctors at Ngaliema Hospital drew samples of Mayinga's blood. Scientists would examine her blood to try to find and identify the mysterious germ that was killing her. The blood was placed in tightly sealed containers and carefully packed. The delicate, deadly cargo was flown to laboratories in Great Britain, Belgium, and the United States. In the United States, the blood was sent to the CDC.

Meanwhile, an international team of epidemiologists headed to Africa. These men and women would search for everyone who had had contact with the Ebola victims. They would probe into the headwaters of the Ebola River looking for the source of the disease. The epidemiologists suspected that the disease was caused by a filovirus, a type of virus that looks like a twisting, looping string. Filoviruses appear to be far more dangerous than other types of viruses.

At the CDC, Dr. Patricia Webb and her husband, Dr. Karl M. Johnson, head of the CDC's Special Pathogens Branch, compared the blood taken from Mayinga with the inventory of blood samples stored at the CDC. Working in a tightly sealed Level 4 laboratory, the scientists identified the virus. This was a new strain, similar to an Ebola virus that had appeared in Sudan, Africa, a few months earlier—though that virus had not been nearly as speedy or deadly a killer. The new strain also resembled the Marburg virus, which had also originated in Africa. Dr. Johnson named the new strain the Zaire strain of the Ebola virus.

Immediately, Dr. Johnson and a team from the CDC were dispatched to Zaire to battle the disease. Meanwhile, the international team of epidemiologists in Kinshasa was locating all persons who had had contact with Mayinga. Remarkably, none of those she had seen outside the hospital, including the boy who shared a soft drink from the same bottle, were ill. But unfortunately, Mayinga died.

In the Bumba Zone, tribal elders put in place a technique they had used over the years to combat other contagious diseases. They separated the sick people from the healthy—a form of quarantine. Villagers who became ill were confined to a hut. No well person could go near them. If the victims survived, that was fine. If they did not survive, they were left in the hut, and the hut and the bodies were burned. By doing this, the villagers were able to stop the spread of Ebola. Two months later, the virus retreated back into the rain forest as mysteriously as it had appeared. The scientists who searched for the source of Ebola did not find it. Since then several outbreaks have occurred in sub-Saharan Africa, one as recently as 2008 in Uganda. This latest outbreak appears to be a new strain of the virus, the source of which remains unknown.

A similar filovirus was eventually discovered in laboratory monkeys at Hazelton Laboratories in Reston, Virginia. Immediately,

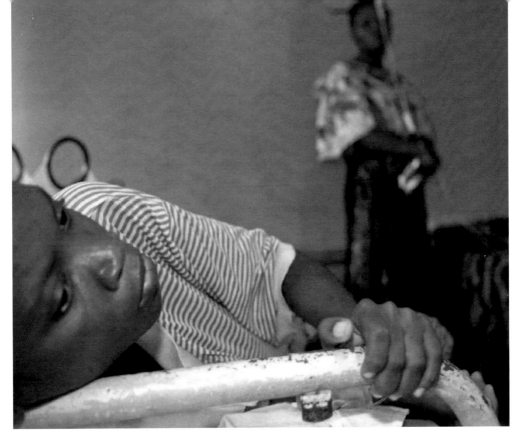

A woman waits in the emergency ward of Kikwit General Hospital in Zaire in May 1995 to find out if she has the Ebola virus.

the U.S. Army Medical Research Institute of Infectious Diseases (USAMRIID) was called in to quarantine the area and destroy the infected monkeys. Officials tracked everyone who had had contact with the infected monkeys.

Apparently, this strain of the virus, the Reston strain, is not harmful to humans. This is very fortunate, because in densely populated areas, viruses can trigger a massive and deadly outbreak. Since the discovery of the Reston strain in 1989, periodic outbreaks have occurred in various parts of the world. The most recent cases among monkeys were in 1996 in the United States and in the Philippines, and no human infections were reported.

(DESERT SCARE)

The place where the boundaries of Colorado, Utah, Arizona, and New Mexico meet is called the Four Corners area. If you stand in the spot where you can touch four states at once, you will see a jagged red desert stretching to the horizon, a land marked by angular peaks and rough canyons. This land is the home of the Navajo Indians.

In May 1993, a healthy twenty-four-year-old Navajo woman from Gallup, New Mexico, suddenly began to gasp for air. She had a high fever and an overwhelming headache. Her family rushed her to a nearby Indian Health Service clinic. But doctors' efforts to save her failed. She died within a few days.

Two days after her death, the woman's boyfriend suffered the same respiratory (lung) ailment while riding in the car with his family on the way to her funeral. Before they could reach medical help, he died. Within the week, two of the woman's neighbors—a young man and a young woman—also died of the same illness.

Something very strange and frightening was happening. At first, doctors suspected bubonic plague, the scourge of the Middle Ages. The plague had appeared from time to time in isolated cases among the Navajos. But no more than one or two cases had occurred at a time, and they had been treated with antibiotics. Dr. Bruce Tempest, a physician with the Indian Health Service, began calling all the clinics on the large Navajo reservation to find out if they had encountered similar cases. He learned that there were indeed other cases of this sudden, deadly respiratory attack.

Dr. Jim Cheek, an epidemiologist with the Indian Health Service, was soon in his laboratory looking under a microscope at slides of fluid samples taken from the five victims. His first

Dr. Beulah Allen of the Indian Health Service hospital was one of many medical experts eager to uncover the mysterious disease that appeared in 1993 among the Navajos.

hunch, too, was that this could be a reemergence of bubonic plague—but the lab reports showed no plague bacteria.

Dr. Cheek continued his detective work. He wondered if the disease could have been caused by exposure to a toxic chemical. His computer search turned up the name of a chemical called phosgene that could have caused the victims' symptoms. Dr. Cheek traveled to the home of one young man who had died and conducted a full search of the trailer where he and his family lived. The entire family had abandoned the trailer, fearing for their lives. There was no trace of the suspected chemical, but the search did reveal an unusually large number of mouse droppings around the trailer, on the floor, and on the shelves.

Dr. Cheek understood what he needed to do to stop an unexplained epidemic. He would have to ask a lot of questions to find the common denominator among the victims. On the other hand, being Native American himself, he could understand the challenges he might encounter in his investigation because of Navajo beliefs about death. Although Dr. Cheek was a Cherokee, he knew that for the Navajos, to speak of the dead or even to say the person's name for many days after the death is taboo. Dr. Cheek realized that there were many questions he could not ask.

At the same time, the Indian Health Service and the state of New Mexico had turned to the CDC for help. Dr. Jay Butler and two of his CDC associates flew to Albuquerque, New Mexico, to coordinate the investigation. Within a day, they had assembled forty colleagues from the New Mexico Department of Health, the University of New Mexico Medical School, and the Indian Health Service. They set out to discover what was causing these deaths.

Meanwhile, another epidemiologist, Dr. Rob Breimen, and his colleagues at the CDC were reviewing the information they had. Their best guess was that the culprit was a virus. To support their theory, they had to eliminate all other possible causes they could identify. Early on, Dr. Cheek had considered the chemical phosgene, which was often used to kill prairie dogs. But after investigating, he found that no one had used this poison in the areas of the outbreak. Further study showed that while exposure to phosgene could produce most of the symptoms of this disease, it did not cause fever. The investigators ruled out phosgene as a cause. Next, they began to try to identify a virus by examining blood samples from the young men and women who had died. They carried out their work in the CDC's levels 3 and 4 laboratories.

Dr. Cheek and Dr. Butler, along with other epidemiologists, began interviewing friends and relatives of those who had died. But information was hard to get because of the taboo against talking about the dead. To make matters more difficult, television and newspaper reporters from all over the country were swarming into the area and producing alarming stories. They called the new disease "Navajo flu," which angered the citizens of the area and made them even more reluctant to talk to outsiders. The publicity caused a mini panic. People began to avoid the Four Corners area, and rumors spread that the Navajo Indians were carriers of a contagious disease.

By June 2, 1993, twelve people had died—and not all were Navajo Indians. The CDC laboratory researchers had grown cultures of viruses taken from blood samples and had begun the matching process. Soon they identified a category of viruses known as hantaviruses as the culprit. But all known hantaviruses caused kidney problems, not lung problems. All the victims had died of respiratory problems. The investigators realized that they were facing something new. Based on what they knew about other hantaviruses, however, they suspected the source of this one to be some type of animal—most likely a rodent.

Dr. Cheek continued his work in New Mexico. Along with the Indian Health Service director and a Navajo doctor, Dr. Cheek sought help from tribal elders and other Navajos. The investigators wanted to know if there were any new tribal practices. Had anyone traveled to other places recently? Had any new foods been brought into the area? Had anyone seen unusual animals or pets in the area? Did anything happen that year that was different from other years?

After asking many questions, the team learned that the piñon nut harvest had been unusually large that year. (Piñon nuts are the edible seeds of the piñon tree, a pine tree common in the southwestern United States.) In turn, the rodent population had increased, since mice and rats thrive on piñons.

The disease detectives went out to gather samples of every

Dr. Jim Cheek, an epidemiologist with the Indian Health Service

type of rodent they could find. More than one hundred scientists, doctors, and animal trappers scoured the Four Corners area searching for clues and gathering a wide assortment of rodents. They drew blood samples from the rodents and shipped the samples to Atlanta for examination.

As the summer wore on, more than twenty thousand rodent blood samples were catalogued. Meanwhile, deaths from the new disease occurred elsewhere in the United States—a grandmother in Texas, a woman in Nevada, and a boy in Oregon. In each case, mouse droppings were discovered near the victims.

Epidemiologists came to believe that the cause of the disease was a new strain of virus carried by deer mice and spread by contact with the droppings of the infected mice. But it was not until the end of 1993 that the microbe was identified as Muerto Canyon virus, named for the canyon on the Navajo reservation where the virus first appeared. *Muerto Canyon* means "valley of death." The disease was stopped from spreading by getting rid of mice and mouse droppings in homes.

CHAPTER SIX

AIDS:
The Modern Pandemic

One of the worst epidemics of all time, AIDS spread around the entire world within twenty years. It is the modern pandemic. AIDS—acquired immunodeficiency syndrome—is caused by the human immunodeficiency virus, or HIV.

Isolated cases of AIDS had probably appeared in central Africa as early as the 1970s, but the HIV virus was not identified until 1984. The first clues appeared in 1981. Dr. Michael Gottlieb, an assistant professor of medicine at the University of California at Los Angeles, noticed five cases of pneumonia among young men whom he saw in his clinical practice.

There were some mystifying things about these cases. First, all the men were homosexual. Second, their pneumonia was caused by a type of parasite that is normally held in check by the body's immune system. In other words, a parasite that was not usually harmful had suddenly become lethal. Dr. Gottlieb also noted that the patients' white blood cell counts were down instead of elevated as they should have been with pneumonia. Dr. Gottlieb reported his findings to the CDC.

Meanwhile, in New York City, Dr. Alvin Friedman-Kien, a dermatologist at New York University Medical School, reported an outbreak of a rare cancer, Kaposi's sarcoma, among young gay men. He also found that their white blood cell counts were down.

Epidemiologists at the CDC believed that they were seeing the beginning of a new epidemic. Although the two diseases were different, they had something important in common: in every case, the patient showed a marked decrease in white blood cells, particularly in one type of white blood cell. These cells, called T cells, act as "commanders" for other parts of the human immune system as it destroys invading microbes.

Normally, if a person has an infection, a blood test will show an increase in the number of white blood cells. In these cases, however, there was a decrease in the number of white blood cells. The immune system did not appear to be working normally. The patients had an immune deficiency. Scientists called the collection of diseases associated with this deficiency acquired immunodeficiency syndrome, or AIDS.

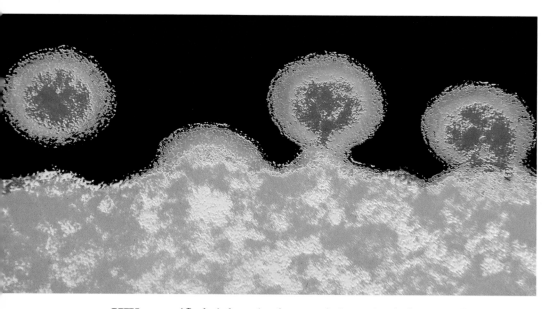

HIV, magnified eighty-six thousand times, buds from a white blood cell (pink).

Dr. Robert Gallo led a team of researchers who identified the virus responsible for AIDS.

At first, the diseases seemed somehow related to homosexuality. But in 1982, the same pattern appeared in people who had had blood transfusions and were not homosexual males. Dr. James Curran, who was monitoring the emerging epidemic from his office at the CDC, traveled to the National Institutes of Health in Bethesda, Maryland, to encourage the researchers there to help investigate this new medical mystery.

His presentation caught the attention of Dr. Robert Gallo, a virologist at the National Cancer Institute, which is head-quartered in Bethesda, Maryland. The suspected culprit was a new microbe. Dr. Gallo and his staff began a search to find the microbe that was causing AIDS. Shortly after reading reports from Dr. Gallo, Dr. Luc Montagnier at the Pasteur Institute in Paris, France, began pursuing the same route of research.

At that time, there were many theories about the cause of AIDS. Some people thought that several diseases were striking the patients at the same time, putting their immune systems into some form of "overload." Others offered a wide range of possible culprits, including Agent Orange, a chemical that was used in the Vietnam War; the wrath of God; an African swine fever released by the Central Intelligence Agency; and a virus manufactured by the U.S. government or the Soviet Union for germ warfare. None of these theories was correct.

For the next two years, researchers working for Dr. Gallo and for Dr. Montagnier tried to find the cause. In April 1984, they found the answer. They called the virus responsible for AIDS the human immunodeficiency virus, or HIV.

With the discovery of HIV, it was possible to begin the process of tracing its origin. In Africa, AIDS was already rampant, but doctors had not recognized it as a distinct syndrome because its victims were dying of a variety of other illnesses, such as cancer and pneumonia. No one had considered that a single virus could be responsible for all these deaths.

Blood tests revealed that as much as 12 percent of the population of the Democratic Republic of Congo (formerly Zaire) carried HIV. Other tests showed that HIV was similar to a virus found in the kidneys of some African green monkeys living in that region. Scientists theorized that the disease, after passing from monkeys to humans, had been carried to Europe by medical personnel working in Africa. It had also traveled to Haiti with Haitians who had worked in Zaire in 1970. From Haiti it appears that the virus traveled to the United States with tourists who had visited Haiti. Over the years, it has spread to countries all over the world, hitting Africa and Asia especially hard.

(HOW HIV WORKS)

The human immune system is an army of millions and millions of white blood cells working with antibodies to fight disease. It is controlled by white blood cells known as helper T cells.

HOW TO PREVENT HIV INFECTION

To prevent the spread of HIV, abstain from sex and do not share intravenous (IV) drug needles. If abstinence from sex is unavoidable, do not participate in behavior that might result in contact with blood, semen, vaginal secretions, or other bodily fluids.

The following are recommended measures to prevent HIV infection:

- Do not have sex with an HIV-infected person.
- Ask about the sexual history of current and future sex partners. Take HIV tests with a potential sex partner.
- Always use a condom during any type of sex (vaginal, anal, or oral). Use latex condoms, and follow the directions on the package.
- Use only water-based lubricants with condoms. Do not use saliva or oil-based lubricants such as petroleum jelly.
- Avoid any sexual practice that could cut the skin and cause bleeding.
- Avoid deep, wet, or "French" kissing with an infected person. A possible cut could occur, which could result in the exchange of blood. It is safe, however, to hug, cuddle, rub, or dry kiss your partner.
- Do not share IV drug needles, syringes, or cookers.
- Do not share personal items such as toothbrushes, razors, or devices used during sex that may be contaminated with bodily fluids.
- If you are infected with HIV, have engaged in high-risk sex, or shared IV drug needles, do not donate blood, plasma, sperm, body organs, or body tissues.

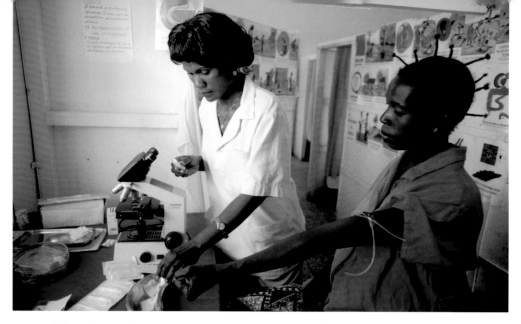

A health worker in the Democratic Republic of Congo takes a blood sample to test for HIV in a patient.

Helper T cells send messages to other white blood cells, directing the fight against invading microbes. One way HIV infects the body is by invading these helper T cells. The virus's DNA changes the DNA in the T cell's control centers, and the T cell begins to produce the virus. Buds of the virus grow from the cell membrane. These buds split off and develop into more viruses, which go on to enter more and more helper T cells.

As HIV takes over helper T cells, the immune system begins to shut down. Without a properly functioning immune system, a person is an easy target for other diseases. Illnesses that are not harmful to a healthy person can kill people with AIDS, because their immune systems are too weak to fight back.

When HIV enters the body, it can remain dormant for up to ten years. Yet it is still infectious. This means that the virus can be transmitted by a person who feels fine and has no visible signs of being sick. It is spread through bodily fluids such as blood and semen. The most common way HIV is transmitted from one person to another is through unprotected sex or by sharing hypodermic needles, a practice that is connected with drug abuse. HIV cannot survive for more than fifteen minutes outside the human body. It is not transmitted on utensils, in food, by food handlers, or by touching.

It is possible to be tested to find out if you have HIV. The two most widely used tests determine if a person's blood contains antibodies to HIV.

(ONGOING EFFORTS)

While there is not yet a vaccine or a cure for HIV/AIDS, some medicines can delay the onset or reduce its intensity. Many people live for years with the disease. At present, combinations of medicines have been developed and are being refined to present a "cocktail" of antiviral drugs to reduce the explosion of HIV in the body. This treatment does not cure AIDS, but it does dramatically slow its progress. The cocktail treatment is a combination of several different drugs referred to as HAART (Highly Active Antiretroviral Therapy). While this therapy has been generally effective in slowing the progress of the virus, doctors have found that these cocktails must be carefully tailored to the individual and to the changing nature of the HIV infection.

The HAART cocktail consists of four main types of medicine: nucleoside reverse transcriptase inhibitors (NRTIs), non-nucleoside reverse transcriptase inhibitors (NNRTIs), protease inhibitors, and fusion inhibitors. The role of these drugs is, first, to block the chemical (enzyme) that HIV needs in order to reproduce itself after it enters the helper T cell; second, to keep the virus from becoming drug resistant; third, to slow the process by which HIV can gain entrance to the target helper T cell; and fourth, to boost the immune system's manufacture of new white blood cells. However, HIV continues to develop drug resistance, requiring careful and periodic medical reassessment and adjustment, and these necessarily powerful drugs can have serious long-term side effects.

In New York, scientists at Cornell University Medical College and at Rockefeller University are taking a different approach. They are investigating the use of umbilical cord blood to create a safe vaccine. B cells (a kind of white blood cell) found in cord blood produce antibodies to a protein that is part of HIV. The scientists hope to use these antibodies to make a vaccine against HIV that does not include HIV itself. This is important because many scientists feel that it would be dangerous to use actual HIV virus, even in a weakened or killed form, in a vaccine.

In an entirely different approach, German researchers at the Max Planck Institute for Molecular Cell Biology and Genetics in Dresden are working in cooperation with the University of Hamburg's Heinrich Pette Institute for Experiment Virology and Immunology. In June 2007, they announced that they had created an enzyme that can sever an HIV viral DNA segment in an HIV infected cell. This action effectively destroys HIV's ability to control its viral reproduction inside of a white blood cell. This technique is referred to as "virus snipping." The scientists in Germany believe that, within the decade, this development could lead to an effective cure for AIDS.

According to the WHO, approximately 33 million people around the world are HIV positive. Thousands more become newly infected every day because the precautions to prevent HIV infection are not understood, are not practiced, or are simply ignored. For these reasons, public health organizations and private philanthropic foundations, such as the Bill & Melinda Gates Foundation of Seattle, Washington, are undertaking worldwide efforts to educate communities about simple and effective precautions. In the autumn of 2007, U.S. president George W. Bush committed the United States to providing billions of dollars to continue the fight against the spread of HIV/AIDS in Africa.

In spite of these international efforts, the AIDS pandemic continues to escalate, particularly in sub-Saharan Africa and in southern and Southeast Asia. According to the Joint United Nations Programme on HIV/AIDS (UNAIDS), 17 million people in these regions are living with AIDS, and in 2007, more than 2 million died of the disease. In contrast, in North America in the same year, about 1 million people were living with AIDS and 50,000 had died.

According to UNAIDS, some countries are taking extreme measures to deal with HIV/AIDS. In these countries, laws have been introduced to make it a crime for a person with an HIV infection (a person can be a carrier of HIV without having developed an active case of AIDS) to expose another person to the virus. No data currently exists to measure the impact on the pandemic of criminalizing HIV transmission, but many public health officials and jurists have voiced the importance of developing strong public health strategies as a more effective alternative to labeling people with HIV/AIDS as criminals.

This concern about the criminalization of HIV/AIDS was highlighted at a special UNAIDS conference held in Geneva, Switzerland, in October 2007. Meanwhile, a variety of new medical and public health approaches offer hope that the pandemic can one day be brought under control and the disease eliminated.

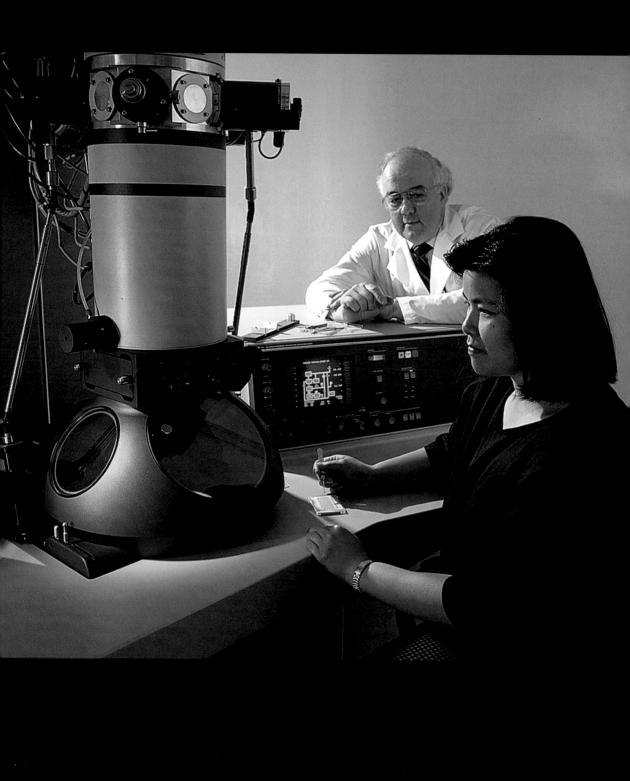

CHAPTERSEVEN
Lyme Disease, Superbugs, and Mad Cow Disease

As the world's growing population crowds into cities with aging water and sewage systems and as we continue to pollute the water we drink and the air we breathe, the conditions are set for new plagues. Modern antibiotics and pesticides also contribute to the emergence of new microbes.

When humans chop down trees to clear land for farms and homes, microbes living in these forests lose their habitats and most find new places to live. Microbes living in animal hosts seek new hosts. If they are able to cross the species barrier to a human host, new diseases can result. Of course, throughout history microbes have moved from animals, birds, or insects to humans, bringing disease. Usually, though, the incidents were isolated, because people lived on farms and in small villages and did not travel far. In modern times, airplanes, ships, trains, and cars carry people, insects, and animals around the world faster and more frequently, sometimes carrying deadly microbes with them. In the early twenty-first century, epidemiologists will continue to rely on basic principles of epidemiology to understand and conquer new and ongoing medical mysteries.

A researcher prepares a slide for viewing on an electron microscope. The microscope uses a focused electron beam to form an image.

(LYME DISEASE)

Most of us think of deer as graceful, gentle creatures. But these animals play a role in the spread of some infectious diseases. Environmental changes on the East Coast of the United States during the last two hundred years helped pave the way for diseases to jump from deer to humans.

In 1975, in the quiet, quaint town of Old Lyme, Connecticut, two children and their parents were suffering with bouts of fever, rashes, headaches, and aching joints. They were diagnosed with rheumatoid arthritis, a disease that causes inflammation, or swelling, of the joints. Usually rheumatoid arthritis affects adults, not children. The juvenile form of the disease is very rare. One of the parents, Polly Murray, learned from her neighbors that other people in the neighborhood, including several children, were also suffering the same symptoms. Murray called the Connecticut State Health Department.

This unusually high number, or cluster, of cases of juvenile rheumatoid arthritis suggested to epidemiologists that something strange was going on. Dr. Allen Steere, an arthritis specialist at the Yale University School of Medicine in New Haven, Connecticut, was called in to investigate. The incidence of juvenile rheumatoid arthritis in Old Lyme was more than one hundred times higher than the normal incidence of the disease in the general population.

Dr. Steere began a systematic search for clues by mapping the location of all reported cases and seeking some commonality among them. He assembled a team of professionals and took them to Old Lyme and the adjoining town of East Haddam. The epidemiologists learned that there had been fifty-one cases of rheumatoid arthritis in 1976, and thirty-nine of the patients were children. They also learned that the disease occurred more often in the summer than in the winter. They suspected that the disease was caused by a microbe that was carried by an insect.

In 1977 Dr. Steere published a scientific paper describing his findings. He gave the new disease the name "Lyme arthritis." So far, he did not know the cause of the disease.

Several people interviewed by epidemiologists remembered that they had been bitten by a small tick before their symptoms began. The doctors dragged cloth bags through the woods to collect ticks for analysis. The ticks were sent to a public health laboratory in Montana that specialized in tick-borne diseases. At this laboratory, Dr. Willy Burgdorfer dissected the ticks and cultured the microbes found in their bodies. He discovered the long, twisting bacterium that caused the arthritic disease. The bacterium was named after the doctor—*Borrelia burgdorferi.*

Borrelia burgdorferi, *the bacterium that causes Lyme disease*

These bacteria live harmlessly in the blood of white-footed deer mice. Immature deer ticks feed on mouse blood and become infected with *Borrelia* bacteria. When a tick reaches adulthood, it feeds on deer. The tick may fall off a deer and end up on a human walking in the woods. Because deer ticks are extremely small—no larger than the period at the end of this sentence—people often don't even realize that they've been bitten.

When a tick bites a human and remains attached for several days to feed, it passes *Borrelia* bacteria into the human's bloodstream as it feeds off the human. At the onset of Lyme disease, a red rash may appear on the skin in a bull's-eye pattern. The person experiences flulike symptoms and later may have pain in the muscles and joints. If the disease is detected early, it is treatable with antibiotics. Untreated, it can lead to a wide range of problems, such as amnesia, changes in behavior, and even fatal heart and respiratory disorders.

Deer ticks (below) *are the vectors, or carriers, of Lyme disease. They are about the size of the period at the end of this sentence.*

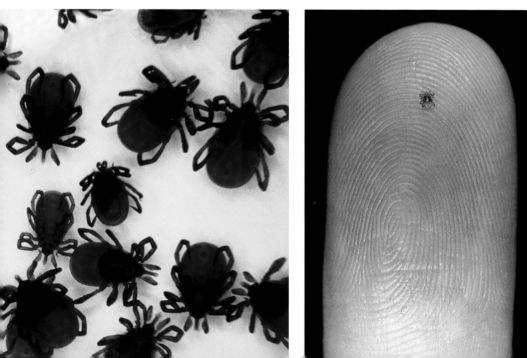

From 1982 to 1996, more than ninety-nine thousand cases of Lyme disease were reported to the CDC. In the United States, Lyme disease is most prevalent in the Northeast, Upper Midwest, and along the Pacific coast.

As the deer population and the human population both increase, the two species are more likely to come into contact with each other. Deer looking for food become bolder, often grazing in suburban backyards.

In 1999 a vaccine against Lyme disease was introduced. The vaccine was given in three doses over a period of one year, and it was only 80 percent effective. The vaccine was recommended only for people between the ages of fifteen and seventy who were at high risk of coming into contact with deer ticks. Because the results were not as expected, the manufacture of the vaccine was discontinued in 2002. Protective measures, such as DEET-based insect repellants and protective clothing, are recommended to avoid the bites that can cause the disease.

(THE SUPERBUGS)

Since bacteria are nothing more than single cells, it seems we should be able to outwit and defeat them. But that is not always the case. As single cells, bacteria can mutate and change their structure to adjust to new circumstances faster than humans can, with our complex organs and our bodies made of millions and millions of cells.

According to the theory of natural selection, organisms that can adapt to meet the challenges of a changing environment are best able to survive and reproduce, ensuring that their offspring will continue to exist. This is also called survival of the fittest. Erasmus Darwin, a physician and naturalist, first proposed these revolutionary ideas about the evolution of plants, animals, and humans in 1790. His grandson, Charles Darwin, set out to test the theory. After finishing his studies in medicine and theology in 1831, Charles Darwin signed up to serve as a naturalist on a British scientific expedition aboard the HMS *Beagle*, a warship converted to serve as his laboratory. During the five years of the journey, Darwin gathered evidence to support his own developing ideas about natural selection. He published his findings in a book called *The Origin of Species.*

Like other creatures, microbes follow the laws of evolution. The fittest survive by making changes to adapt to new conditions. The hosts upon which microbes depend also change. The hosts' immune systems adapt and find ways to destroy the microbial invaders. These changes do not happen suddenly, however. In 1994 science writer Laurie Garrett described the process of mutation in her book, *The Coming Plague: Newly Emerging Diseases in a World Out of Balance*: "Roughly one out of every 10 million *E. coli* [bacteria] in a petri dish might randomly mutate to be resistant to, say, penicillin. Then, if the drug were poured into the petri dish, 9,999,999 bacteria would die, but that one resistant *E. coli* would survive, and divide and multiply, passing the genes for resistance on to its progeny."

The staphylococcus family of bacteria have shown a remarkable ability to become resistant to antibiotics. While staph bacteria live harmlessly on the skin of most people, the bacteria can cause a wide range of problems. These problems include boils, pneumonia, urinary tract infection, toxic shock syndrome, and arthritis. Infections from this family of bacteria are called staph infections.

In 1952 most staph infections were easily treated by the antibiotic penicillin. Forty years later, penicillin could cure only 10 percent of staph infections in developed nations. This is

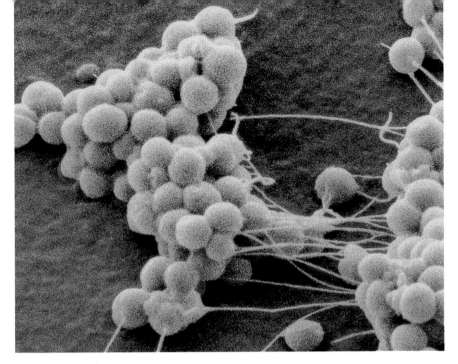

Some strains of staphylococcus bacteria, shown here magnified 3,145 times, have become resistant to certain antibiotics. This has become a major concern among health professionals.

because strains of staphylococcus bacteria developed resistance to penicillin—they mutated and avoided being killed by the drug. Doctors began using other antibiotics, but staph bacteria have slowly become resistant to each new antibiotic. Epidemiologists fear that a new strain of staph will emerge that will be resistant to all available antibiotics. Several other bacterial diseases are also developing antibiotic resistance.

Several factors have contributed to the development of antibiotic resistance in bacteria. First, antibiotics have been widely used as a general cure-all, sometimes even when they are unnecessary, such as in the treatment of a viral infection. (Antibiotics are effective against bacteria, but not viruses.) This widespread use of antibiotics has allowed bacteria to "hurry" the process of natural selection. And antibiotics are not always taken properly. Say, for example, a doctor prescribes penicillin to a patient with a strep throat infection. The patient takes the medicine for a few days, feels better, and then stops taking it before using the prescribed amount. The problem is that all the bacteria may not have been killed. Those remaining are the "fittest." They form the beginning of a drug-resistant strain.

Second, in poorer countries, antibiotics are used for a variety of purposes—often unrelated to a drug's intended use—and without proper control. Bacteria mutate and develop resistance to the antibiotics. These superbugs move to different parts of the world as people travel.

Third, modern hospitals provide bacteria with an ideal breeding ground. More antibiotics are used in hospitals than anywhere else. Many people who come to the hospital are already sick, with weakened immune systems, so they are more susceptible to germs. If bacteria that are resistant to one antibiotic come in contact with bacteria that are resistant to another antibiotic, some of the bacteria may become resistant to both drugs.

In hospitals, staphylococcus bacteria are common. They can pass from person to person by contact or by touching the same utensils. In 1992 nearly one million people who underwent surgery in the United States suffered a postsurgical infection, even though hospitals uphold stringent standards for cleanliness in the operating room. An infection that develops in a hospital or other health-care facility is called a nosocomial infection. Many of these infections are staph infections.

Soon after antibiotics were developed to treat human bacterial diseases, veterinarians and livestock producers began to use these same medicines to treat animals. Not only were antibiotics used to treat sick animals, but they were also given to cows, chickens, pigs, and sheep on a regular basis to keep them healthier.

THE MOBILITY OF GENES

Each bacterium contains its own strands of DNA. The DNA instructions for building more, identical microbes are encoded in chromosomes— long strings of molecular beads containing thousands of genes. Genes control the expression and transmission of specific traits of an organism. As bacteria multiply and reproduce, genes from one bacterium are passed to the next.

In the 1940s and 1950s, geneticist Barbara McClintock (*right*) did experiments with corn plants at the Cold Spring Harbor Laboratory on Long Island, New York, to learn more about how genes work. She found that some genes were mobile—they

could move within strands of DNA. When a gene changed from one place on its chromosome to another, the result was a radical change in the appearance of the corn.

Other scientists built on McClintock's work and discovered that the principle of genetic mobility also applied to other organisms, including bacteria. The mobility of genes gives bacteria another tool for developing resistance to antibiotics.

The health of farm animals did improve. At the same time, new strains of bacteria developed that were resistant to antibiotics.

In February 1993, Dr. Michael Osterholm, the Minnesota state epidemiologist, noticed an increase in the number of food poisoning cases in Minnesota. He traced the problem to a bacterium called *Salmonella newport*. Salmonella bacteria cause diarrhea and vomiting in humans. These flulike symptoms are usually referred to as food poisoning. Dr. Osterholm noticed two strange things about these cases. The newport form of salmonella was native to the southern states near the Gulf of Mexico, far from Minnesota. He also noted that the people who fell ill with this form of salmonella poisoning were sicker than would normally be expected and the bacteria seemed resistant to four different antibiotics.

Dr. Osterholm began an epidemiological investigation. He sent notices to other health departments around the country. He learned that there had been similar outbreaks in North and South Dakota. Each of the victims had eaten a hamburger before falling ill. Further investigation turned up 40,000 pounds (18,144 kg) of contaminated beef. The Minnesota Department of Health traced the beef to a herd of cattle that had been given antibiotics. Antibiotic-resistant salmonella bacteria had developed in these cattle, and the bacteria had passed to people who had eaten meat from the cattle.

(MAD COW DISEASE)

Humans face a wide range of microbes, including viruses, bacteria, and parasites. Recently, what may be a new disease-causing agent was discovered—the prion, an infectious particle of protein. Not all scientists agree that prions exist. The theory of prions stems from the study of several diseases, including one found among a tribe on a remote jungle island.

The island nation of Papua New Guinea lies in the Pacific Ocean, north of Australia, and stretches for 1,500 miles (2,430 km) east to west. High in the mountains, protected by heavy rain forests, Melanesian farmers live in much the same way as their Stone Age ancestors did, without electricity or running water.

One of the Melanesian tribes is the Fore. Fore women traditionally had the task of preparing bodies for burial. They removed and handled the brains, and sometimes they ate pieces of the brains, giving some to their children. This practice, they believed, would give them strength and wisdom.

Some Fore people developed a terrible illness. First, they began to stagger when walking. Then they could not walk at all. Victims had trouble swallowing, and they died shivering and shaking. The Fore called this syndrome kuru, the trembling sickness. They believed that kuru was caused by evil spirits.

In 1957 Dr. D. Carleton Gajdusek, a young U.S. pediatrician and virologist, heard about this mysterious trembling sickness. Based on the symptoms, he suspected that it might be a new disease, a new form of brain infection. Dr. Gajdusek wanted to investigate. He went into the jungle highlands of Papua New Guinea and hiked from village to village, asking questions and collecting blood and tissue samples.

Dr. Gajdusek didn't know whether the disease was genetic or if it was caused by an infectious microbe or some other agent. He wanted to autopsy the brains of people who had died of kuru to see if he could find out what caused the disease. He traded axes and tobacco for brains of dead Fore members. He saw no sign of a viral or bacterial infection in the brain tissue. But he did notice microscopic, tangled knots of protein known as amyloid plaques. These plaques are more commonly seen in people with Alzheimer's disease, a disease of aging marked by mental deterioration. The symptoms and results of kuru were most similar to those of a rare brain disease called Creutzfeldt-Jakob disease (CJD). In both kuru and CJD, the brain becomes "spongy," or full of holes, causing mental and physical deterioration in the victim.

Dr. Gajdusek believed there had to be some virus that was transmitting kuru, but he could not find an infective agent. He was able to reproduce the disease in laboratory monkeys by inoculating them with kuru-infected tissue. This suggested that the Fore people could have been infected through cuts in their hands when they touched the brains of kuru victims, or they became infected by eating the brains.

By the 1960s, the government of Papua New Guinea began to enforce a ban on cannibalism among the Fore. As the Fore people abandoned the custom of eating brains, the new generation of children was mostly free of any sign of kuru.

In 1976 Dr. Gajdusek was awarded the Nobel Prize in Medicine for his research on kuru. Two years later, Dr. Stanley Prusiner, a biochemist and neurologist, traveled to Papua New Guinea to help Dr. Gajdusek look for the mysterious virus. Dr. Prusiner hoped to discover the cause of Creutzfeldt-Jakob disease, which he associated with a disease called scrapie, which caused brain damage in sheep.

By 1982 Dr. Prusiner was ready to present a scientific paper on his research. He declared that the cause of scrapie was an infectious protein, which he named a prion. This was, he said, an infectious protein particle containing no nucleic acid. In 1997 Dr. Prusiner was awarded a Nobel Prize for his research.

No one has ever seen a prion, even with an electron microscope. Some scientists are skeptical of the concept. Some people think these "spongy brain" diseases may be caused by a primitive kind of virus called a virino.

In 1986, as research into the cause of scrapie and kuru continued, an epidemic struck cattle in Britain. Cows with this fatal disease changed personality. They became aggressive, nervous, and hard to handle. They lost their coordination and began to stumble. Whole herds were affected. Newspaper headlines called the syndrome mad cow disease. The official name of the disease is bovine spongiform encephalopathy (BSE).

Epidemiologists were called in. What did two hundred cows from different parts of Britain have in common? The only common factor was their feed. The cows were given a high protein mixture that included rendered sheep—slaughtered sheep that had been ground up and processed. This food included the remains of sheep that had died of scrapie.

In 1995 Dr. James Ironside, a pathologist with the British National CJD Surveillance Unit in Edinburgh, Scotland, found amyloid plaques and spongelike holes in the brain tissue of a teenage boy who had died of Creutzfeldt-Jakob disease. Spongy holes were also the major feature of kuru and scrapie. Dr. Ironside alerted the director of the surveillance unit, Dr. Robert Will, who turned up more cases of CJD. By the end of 1996, ten cases had appeared. At first, the patients acted "nutty" and then slowly, over months, they began to stagger, tremble, and ultimately die. Epidemiologists feared that an infectious agent had spread from cattle to humans when people ate beef from BSE-infected cattle.

The British cabinet convened emergency sessions of Parliament, the highest legislative body of Great Britain. On March 19, 1996, Stephen Dorrell, the secretary of state for Health,

On May 14, 1996, the World Health Organization held a meeting of experts to discuss Creutzfeldt-Jakob disease and mad cow disease.

stood in the House of Commons and announced to Parliament and the world that BSE might have spread from cattle to humans in the form of Creutzfeldt-Jakob disease. In the United States, the Food and Drug Administration issued regulations to protect Americans from the possible spread of mad cow disease. The regulations forbade the use of slaughtered and processed animals in food for cows, sheep, or goats. Only two cases of BSE have been identified in cows in the United States, one in 2003 and the other in 2005. Meat from the two cows did not enter the human food supply. In Britain the number of BSE-infected cattle declined sharply because of tough rules regulating farms. Scientists still do not know whether the causative agent of these spongiform diseases is a prion, a slow-acting virus, a virino, or some new form of microbe.

CHAPTEREIGHT
Bioterrorism

Bioterrorism is the use of deadly germs to kill or terrorize an enemy. The word is a relatively recent addition to the En-glish language, but the concept has been around for thousands of years.

Without having any concept of "germs," warriors in many ancient civilizations engaged in acts of bioterrorism. Both the Greeks and the Romans threw carcasses of diseased animals into their enemies' water supplies to spread disease and death. The Muslim warriors who catapulted dead plague victims over the walls of Caffa in the 1300s were also bioterrorists.

The first documented biological warfare in American history took place during the French and Indian War (1754–1763). Lord Jeffrey Amherst, commander of the British forces in North America, suggested the use of smallpox as a weapon against the Native Americans. When the disease broke out at Fort Pitt (modern Pittsburgh) in 1763, smallpox-infected blankets were given to warriors from a local Native American tribe. The gift was followed by an epidemic among the tribes along the Ohio River, killing half of their population.

When Japan invaded Manchuria in the early 1930s, it began a biological warfare research program using Chinese prisoners as guinea pigs. From 1932 until the end of World War II in 1945, Japan operated an infamous research facility code-named Unit 731. During the thirteen years that this program was in operation, more than ten thousand prisoners died of experimental infections or direct execution. Unit 731 also conducted large-scale experiments. In one, plague-infected fleas were released from airplanes flying over Chinese cities to cause epidemics of bubonic plague.

Also during World War II, a U.S. biological warfare research program was begun at Fort Detrick (then Camp Detrick) in Maryland. The work continued after the war ended.

In 1972 more than one hundred nations, including the United States, Iraq, and the Soviet Union, signed the Biological Weapons Convention. This treaty prohibited the development and use of biological weapons. Despite the treaty, the Soviet Union and Iraq each continued to develop biological weapons. The Russian program, Biopreparat, had the capacity to produce large quantities of smallpox, plague, and anthrax microbes.

Although nations such as Russia, Iran, Iraq, Syria, and North Korea continued to develop biological weapons, none has actually used these weapons in an attack. Rather, small groups and individuals have become the bioterrorists. For example, in 1984 followers of Indian guru Bhagwan Shree Rajneesh intentionally contaminated salad bars in ten restaurants in The Dalles, Oregon, with salmonella bacteria, causing 751 people to fall ill. The purpose of the assault was to test the cult's biowarfare techniques. The outbreak brought large numbers of epidemiologists to The Dalles, making further attacks impossible.

(POTENTIAL WEAPONS FOR BIOWARFARE)

The CDC has identified eighteen classes of diseases that are the most likely to be used in biowarfare. Only a handful of these would be effective on a large scale. For a microbe to be used as an agent of mass destruction, it must cause illness or death, a delivery system must be available, and the public must not be immune to it. Anthrax, smallpox, tularemia, and botulism and, to a lesser extent, bubonic plague and viral hemorrhagic fevers are the microbes most likely to be used by bioterrorists.

Anthrax is the bioterrorist weapon of choice. A small amount can easily be used to cause widespread danger and disruption. If the symptoms are quickly recognized and diagnosed by health authorities, however, such an outbreak can be contained.

The first anthrax attack on the United States came as a surprise. On October 5, 2001, Robert Stevens, a photo editor for a tabloid publishing company in Boca Raton, Florida, died of inhalation anthrax. A mailroom clerk in the same publishing house was also diagnosed with anthrax, but he recovered.

Following the diagnosis of inhalation anthrax in Florida, the CDC was on high alert. At first, natural causes were assumed. But then an NBC employee in New York City was diagnosed with cutaneous anthrax after she opened a letter containing a powdery substance. It became clear that bioterrorists were responsible. Within days the largest force of disease detectives ever assembled began investigating the anthrax attacks.

Soon two more anthrax-laced letters appeared, one addressed to the U.S. Senate majority leader, Thomas Daschle of South Dakota and the other to Senator Patrick Leahy of Vermont. These letters had been processed at the Brentwood mail distribution center in Washington, D.C. Anthrax spores leaked from the letters during handling, contaminating other mail and exposing postal workers to the attack.

Health officials closed several buildings for fumigation. Tens of thousands of letters were shipped to Ohio for irradiation to kill anthrax spores. Thousands of postal workers and

Hazardous materials unit workers take turns hosing one another down. The unit is inspecting government buildings in Washington, D.C., for anthrax contamination during the October 2001 anthrax scare.

government office workers were examined for the presence of anthrax and given a sixty-day regimen of the antibiotic ciprofloxacin.

At-risk workers were also offered an as-yet-unlicensed anthrax vaccine. By the time the emergency was over, a few spore-filled letters had indirectly affected thousands of people, disrupted government and commerce, and directly infected at least eleven people with inhalation anthrax, killing five.

The use of a smallpox virus as an agent of terrorism has become an ominous possibility. Routine smallpox vaccinations were discontinued in the United States in 1972 and worldwide in 1984. Because immunity due to vaccination decreases over time, even those who were vaccinated may have lost their immunity. There is a limited supply of smallpox vaccine and no effective cure. After the 2001 anthrax attacks, the U.S. government began a massive program to produce millions of vials of vaccine to be ready for a terrorist attack involving smallpox.

If smallpox microbes were sprayed into the air and infected only fifty to one hundred people, the disease could spread person-to-person to thousands of people within weeks. Quick diagnosis, immediate identification of the source of the virus, complete quarantine of all contacted persons, and a well-organized vaccination plan would be necessary to contain the outbreak.

Botulism is caused by a bacterium, *Clostridium botulinum*, which produces botulinum toxin, one of nature's deadliest poisons. Botulism is principally associated with improperly prepared or handled foods. Any airborne delivery of botulism bacteria would signal a bioterrorist attack. Iran, Iraq, North Korea, and Syria have developed or at one time were believed to have developed botulinum toxin as a weapon, as well as methods to deploy it.

Tularemia, or rabbit fever, is a highly infectious disease caused by the bacterium *Francisella tularensis*. In nature, tularemia is carried by rodents, rabbits, and hares that have been infected by ticks, flies, or mosquitoes. The disease is transmitted to humans who are bitten by infected ticks or insects, handle infected animals, or drink contaminated water. It is not transmitted from person to person. Because of the low natural incidence of tularemia, any sudden outbreak would be suspected of being caused by bioterrorists.

Bubonic plague and viral hemorrhagic fevers (VHFs) are also possible candidates for bioterrorist use. VHFs are caused by several different families of viruses. Some of these diseases are relatively mild, but others, such as Ebola hemorrhagic fever, are life threatening. VHFs are naturally found in animal hosts but can be transmitted to humans. Some VHFs can also be transmitted from human to human. Plague and VHFs are harder to incorporate into attack mechanisms and harder to control once released than anthrax, smallpox, tularemia, or botulism, so they are not as attractive to bioterrorists. The threat of these diseases is not, however, overlooked by the organizations focused upon protecting the United States from the military use of deadly microbes.

(BIOTERRORISM AND EPIDEMIOLOGISTS)

Bioterrorism presents the greatest challenge to epidemiologists. In the wake of the 2001 al-Qaeda terrorist attacks in the United States, the CDC urged heightened surveillance. Healthcare professionals must immediately report cases of any of the potential bioterrorism diseases to the epidemiological centers in their state or directly to the CDC.

Likely the first warning of any clandestine bioterrorist attack would be a sudden, unusual cluster of cases of one of the suspect diseases. Because there is a delay between exposure to a terrorist's release of microbes and the actual outbreak of a disease in a population, time is critical. Unusual patterns of disease must be considered with great suspicion and met with a rapid response. This is the role of disease detectives in the United States.

CHAPTER NINE
Ongoing Battles:
Avian Flu, West Nile Virus, and SARS

In May 1997, in the New Territories of Hong Kong, a three-year-old boy died a painful death of respiratory failure. He was diagnosed with influenza, but the identified virus did not match any known flu virus. Realizing that they were facing a potentially deadly but unknown type of flu virus and fearing the possibility of a new disease outbreak, Chinese public health doctors began to trace the boy's activities prior to his illness.

Their investigation led them to a day-care center where the boy and other children had played with baby chicks provided by their caregivers to entertain the children. When the doctors learned that the baby chicks had been dying, they suspected flu. It was known that, from time to time, chickens, ducks, geese, and other fowl died when an avian influenza virus raced through their flocks. When tests revealed that the dead boy had suffered from the same virus, they realized that avian flu—once restricted solely to birds—had leaped to humans.

Flu can spread rapidly on droplets of water through coughing, sneezing, touching hand to mouth, or through touching hand to hand to mouth. For this reason, public health officials feared that the new mutation of the avian flu passing from fowl to people could easily begin an epidemic. Reacting quickly, Chinese officials enlisted the aid of more than two thousand volunteers to cull chickens in chicken farms, yards, and live-chicken markets, slaughtering and destroying millions of chickens to halt the spread of the disease. Although many people fell ill and six more people died, the destruction of chickens on a mass scale succeeded in avoiding a local epidemic.

However, chickens are not the only carriers of avian flu. Moving flocks carried the virus throughout Southeast Asia. Within a few years, avian flu had infected more than 100 million chickens, geese, ducks, and other fowl and had spread to humans in Cambodia, Thailand, Vietnam, Indonesia, other areas of China, and three other countries in eastern Asia. Although the virus is virulent, its human-to-human transmission appeared to be limited to transmissions from humans handling live or dead infected birds in open markets. Still epidemiologists around the world feared that this mutation of the virus had the potential for a worldwide pandemic. They watched Asia closely.

In Vietnam a program to vaccinate certain flocks of chickens and ducks limited the spread of the disease among the birds there. Meanwhile, avian flu began to appear in parts of Eastern Europe. The World Health Organization met in Geneva to develop an information and virus-sharing plan for all the attending nations. In the United States, in 2005 President George W. Bush launched an International Partnership on Avian and Pandemic Influenza in cooperation with the New Delhi Ministerial Conference on Avian and Pandemic Influenza. As a result of

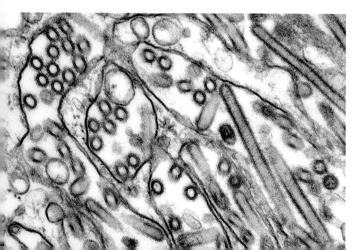

This colored electron micrograph shows avian flu virus (seen in gold) in cells.

Indonesian workers carry chickens to slaughter after two people died from avian flu in that country in March 2007.

this conference in India, eight nations and the European Commission (the executive branch of the European Union) jointly pledged $605 million to fight against a potential pandemic. In April 2006, with outbreaks of avian flu among domestic fowl continuing to occur, President Bush allocated billions of dollars to prepare U.S. health-care providers and epidemiologists with the means to monitor and confront potential outbreaks.

By December 2007, avian flu in birds and in humans had spread into the Middle East and Africa (Egypt and Nigeria) but not into the Americas. Since the disease remains an ongoing threat, the CDC is working with the World Health Organization to closely monitor the situation. Additionally, the CDC is partnering with WHO and the National Institutes of Health to develop a vaccine.

(WEST NILE VIRUS)

You might think that the West Nile virus earned its name from the Nile River in Egypt. In studies conducted there in the 1950s, the relationship between birds, mosquitoes (which carry the virus), and people was first understood. However, the virus itself was first isolated earlier in the treatment of a fever-ridden woman in the West Nile District of Uganda to the south and east of Egypt and from there derives its name. From Africa, West Nile virus spread to Eastern Europe, the Middle East, Asia, and finally to the United States.

At the beginning of the summer of 1999, an unusual number of dead and dying crows were noted in Queens, one of New York's five boroughs. By midsummer, blood specimens had been sent to the CDC for identification. The CDC identified the virus as West Nile virus, which they matched with an identical virus from a brain specimen from a case of human encephalitis (acute inflammation of the brain). By late summer 1999, there was a cluster of cases of viral encephalitis in the New York–Connecticut area along with a noticeable number of dead or dying crows. Tests revealed that the birds were carrying the West Nile virus. Since that date, mosquitoes and infected birds have carried the virus rapidly westward. By 2004 it has spread into most of the lower forty-eight states.

Disease detectives collected and reported the location of dead crows throughout the country, with local health authorities conveying their observations to the CDC. As Dr. William Reisen, professor at the Department of Pathology at the University of California School of Veterinary Medicine in Davis, California, explained, "Crows are more susceptible to the virus than other specimens of birds. There's an amazing amount of virus in the blood stream of infected crows. Sometimes as much as 10 billion viruses in one millimeter [0.04 inch] of blood."

West Nile virus is an arbovirus, a large group of viruses spread through blood-feeding insects such as mosquitoes. Mosquitoes bite and draw blood from an infected bird and then pass on the infection to any other bird, animal, or human that they bite. In

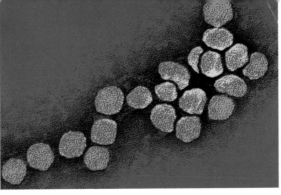

Left: *A scientist prepares to take samples from a dead crow at a laboratory at the University of Connecticut in September 1999. The crow was being tested to see if it had died of West Nile virus.*

Above: *An electron micrograph of West Nile virus*

the animal kingdom, the horse is the most severely affected by West Nile virus. A horse with West Nile virus loses coordination, stumbles, grows weak with twitching muscles and, in a severe case, can no longer stand. Thirty percent of horses bitten by a mosquito carrying West Nile virus will die.

Humans, on the other hand, face a lesser risk of infection. In areas where there is West Nile virus exposure, fewer that 1 percent of the mosquitoes carry the virus, and from among those people who are bitten by an infected mosquito, fewer than 1 percent become severely ill. Some people infected with the virus will show no symptoms. Others may experience a skin rash, headache, fever, diarrhea, nausea, back and muscle aches, lack of appetite, and fatigue in varying degrees of severity. Some people, however, can suffer a potentially fatal inflammation, with swelling of the membrane enclosing the brain (encephalitis) or of the spinal cord (meningitis).

A West Nile virus vaccine is available for horses, although there is not a vaccine for humans at this time. The recommended protection against the virus is the use of DEET-based insect re-pellents, wearing long-sleeved shirts and long pants, and other general precautions for avoiding mosquitoes and their bites.

(SEVERE ACUTE RESPIRATORY SYNDROME)

A public health cover-up of a new and unexplained disease can lead to disaster. This occurred in November 2002, when a farmer from Foshan, Guangdong (formerly Canton), in southern China was rushed to the hospital with a high fever, stomach problems, cough, and sore throat. The initial diagnosis was flu. In the hospital, the farmer developed breathing problems with pneumonia-like symptoms. Before a diagnosis could be made, he died. The health authorities were unsure of what had caused the death. They made no report to the World Health Organization to enlist international help. Within three months three hunded more people in China had become ill with the same disease, and five had died.

Chinese officials issued no warning of the newly developing disease. Yet rumors began to leak out of China that the nation was facing a new epidemic. A new and unknown coronavirus (named for the virus's corona, a halolike structure visible under the microscope) had emerged from the animal kingdom and was bringing a potentially deadly viral pneumonia to people. Official China remained silent.

Canada Global Public Health Intelligence Network, a part of the World Health Organization, picked up news of the rumor. The network believed that a new type of flu was beginning to circulate in China. WHO officials asked for information from China but got no reply.

Finally, Dr. Jiang Yanyong, a retired Chinese army surgeon, defied authorities and reported the new virus to WHO. Top

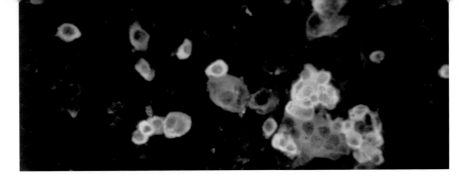

This microscopic image shows human cells (darker green) being infected with SARS (lighter green).

Chinese leaders reluctantly admitted that they had been giving false reports and that hundreds of Chinese were dying of this new illness. (Dr. Jiang was later awarded the 2007 Heinz R. Pagels Human Rights of Scientists Award for his selfless work to contain the epidemic. Yet his superiors, angry at his exposure of the SARS epidemic, denied him the right to leave China to travel to New York to receive the prize.)

The new virus was finally identified as a mutation of a coronavirus, which can spread through direct human contact and in the water particles of coughs and sneezes. The name of the new disease—severe acute respiratory syndrome, or SARS—came from the medical symptoms associated with the illness.

In March 2003, WHO issued a global SARS alert, but it was too late. The virus had already begun to reach around the world, carried by unsuspecting air travelers. Outbreaks appeared in twenty-six countries, including the United States. By the end of July, more than eight thousand people had become ill and more than seven hundred deaths had resulted from SARS. The majority of the cases were in China.

Also, in 2003, WHO requested eleven laboratories in nine countries to participate in a coordinated research effort to identify the cause of SARS. People in China often live in close proximity with their animals, particularly poor people in crowded cities, on farms, and in marketplaces where a wide range of

A health worker uses an infrared gun to measure the body temperature of a traveler at an airport in China in 2004. Chinese officials stepped up checks at airports and other locations after a SARS case was reported earlier that year.

animals are offered as food. For this reason, zoonosis was suspected. Zoonotic diseases are those that pass from animals to humans. The suspicion was correct, as the Chinese horseshoe bat was finally identified as the original carrier of this virus.

In parts of China, bats and civets (a catlike animal found in Asia and Africa) are sources of food. The civets may have become infected by bats and then carried the virus into marketplaces where both bats and civets are sold for food.

In the United States, the CDC moved quickly to locate and contain potential outbreaks. They issued health alert notices to travelers who journeyed in those areas where they might be exposed to cases of SARS. The CDC also offered assistance to state and local health departments and performed around-the-clock surveillance.

Because doctors were alerted to the new syndrome, they were able to make early diagnoses and to quickly isolate and quarantine sick patients. As a result, the virus did not get a chance to enlarge its reach. Then, as mysteriously as it had arrived, the SARS virus disappeared. Epidemiologists, however, are keeping a careful eye on the virus in order to be ready for any new outbreaks.

CONCLUSION
Epidemiology and the Future

Infectious disease epidemiologists are our sentinels, guarding against some of humanity's most dangerous enemies—microbes. These minuscule organisms have caused more harm to more people throughout history than all wars combined.

One hundred years ago, deaths from infectious diseases were still commonplace all over the world. By the end of World War II, however, scientists had an array of weapons for battling microbes—antibiotics, vaccinations, and improved sanitation. Many diseases, such as whooping cough and diphtheria, had practically disappeared. The great plagues that had ravaged whole populations—smallpox, typhus, typhoid fever, and measles—had been virtually conquered. Following the United States' lead, other countries began to use DDT and other pesticides to control mosquitoes and prevent the spread of malaria. By the 1960s, most Americans believed that modern science had brought the threat of epidemics to an end.

While we were "conquering" disease, bacteria and viruses were quietly evolving and adapting. Microbes are not smarter than we are, but they have been around much longer. They are also less complex, so they can mutate and evolve faster than we can. Bacteria that have survived death by antibiotics become superbugs, resistant to our most powerful drugs. Viruses change their shape to survive. Some of our old enemies are returning with a vengeance.

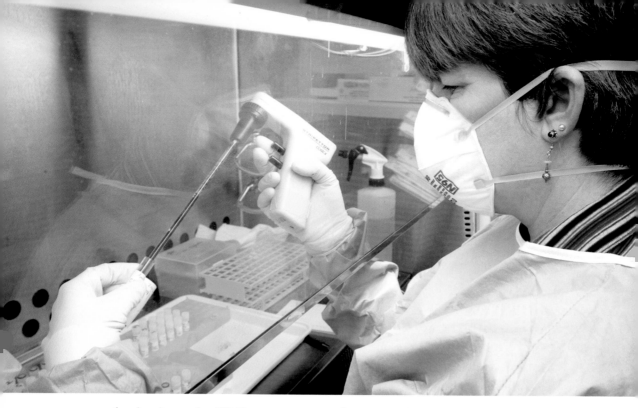

A scientist at the CDC processes a specimen containing SARS. Disease detectives around the world collaborate with the World Health Organization to try to stop the spread of disease.

Because of environmental changes and human mobility, new epidemics such as AIDS have spread around the globe. Tuberculosis is on the rise again, and new outbreaks of ancient epidemics—cholera, malaria, yellow fever, diphtheria, and influenza—are making headlines again. Deadly viruses such as Ebola have leaped out of their jungle habitats.

Still, the remarkable skills of disease detectives help to prevent widespread medical disasters. Their understanding of how diseases spread helps keep us safe from our invisible enemies. While the danger of microbial invasion is real, epidemiologists are watching for signs of an epidemic and are ready to take action to stop the threat.

GLOSSARY

AIDS (acquired immunodeficiency syndrome): a collection of diseases caused by the human immunodeficiency virus (HIV), which attacks and destroys the helper T cells of the immune system

anthrax: a disease caused by the bacterium *Bacillus anthracis*. It primarily affects plant-eating animals such as cattle and sheep, but it can be transmitted to humans.

antibiotics: medicines used to treat bacterial infections

antibodies: molecular proteins that attack and destroy specific microbes that invade the human body

arbovirus: a virus that is spread through blood-feeding insects such as mosquitoes

avian influenza: an influenza virus found chiefly in birds. It is usually fatal to domestic fowl and can sometimes infect humans.

bacteria: single-celled microorganisms that live in soil, water, plants, animals, and humans and can cause disease

bioterrorism: the use of deadly germs to kill or terrorize an enemy

botulism: a disease usually associated with improperly prepared or handled foods; caused by the *Clostridium botulinum* bacterium

bovine spongiform encephalopathy (BSE): a disease that affects cattle, causing their brains to have a spongelike appearance and resulting in loss of coordination due to brain damage; also called mad cow disease

bubonic plague: a disease caused by the *Yersinia pestis* bacterium, spread by fleas from rats, which caused widespread death during the Middle Ages; also called Black Death

cholera: a disease caused by *Vibrio cholerae* bacteria, which live in contaminated water. Cholera causes severe diarrhea, vomiting, and fever and is often fatal.

coronavirus: a virus that, under a high-powered microscope, reveals a unique corona, or halolike structure

Creutzfeldt-Jakob disease (CJD): a fatal, progressive degeneration of the brain characterized by lack of coordination, seizures, confusion, and spongelike (spongiform) formations in the brain

culture: nutrients used to grow microorganisms in a laboratory

diphtheria: an infectious, often fatal disease that causes swelling of the throat and tonsils, difficulty breathing, and high fever; caused by the *Corynebacterium diphtheriae* bacterium

DNA (deoxyribonucleic acid): a molecule in the nuclei of cells that contains instructions determining the characteristics of organisms

Ebola: a family of viruses that cause deadly hemorrhagic diseases (diseases characterized by internal bleeding)

epidemic: an unusually high incidence of a disease or illness among a community of people

epidemiology: the study of disease and health in populations

filovirus: a type of virus that looks like a twisting, looping string

fungi: spore-producing organisms that lack chlorophyll, usually classified as plants. There are over one hundred thousand species of fungi, including yeasts, molds, smuts, and mushrooms.

hantaviruses: a family of viruses that cause hemorrhagic fever diseases, usually characterized by fever, weakness, fatigue, internal bleeding, and kidney failure. These viruses are carried by rodents.

HIV (human immunodeficiency virus): the virus that causes acquired immunodeficiency syndrome (AIDS)

immune system: the units of the body, especially white blood cells, that work together to fight disease

immunity: resistance to a disease

infection: the reproduction of microbes in the body

infectious diseases: illnesses that can be spread or transmitted

influenza: a viral disease resulting in high fever, muscle aches, chest congestion, and intestinal irritation; usually called the flu

kuru: a disease found among members of the Fore tribe in Papua New Guinea. Symptoms begin with shivering, followed by loss of the ability to walk and swallow, and finally death.

Legionnaires' disease: a lung infection caused by the *Legionnella pneumophila* bacterium

Lyme disease: a disease caused by the *Borrelia burgdorferi* bacterium and spread by the bite of the deer tick

malaria: a disease that occurs in tropical and subtropical regions and is spread through the bite of female *Anopheles* mosquitoes

microbes: the general term applied to organisms, such as bacteria and viruses, that are too small to be seen by the naked eye

Muerto Canyon virus: a hantavirus that spreads through contact with dust from the feces of deer mice

mutate: to undergo a change in molecular structure that is continued in succeeding generations of the organism

pandemic: an epidemic that spreads to an entire country or continent or to the whole world

parasites: organisms that feed on or live in other organisms

prion: thought to be an infectious protein with no nucleic acid

protozoa: single-celled microscopic organisms. Some are parasites.

quarantine: isolation of a person or group of people suspected of being infected with a disease to prevent the spread of that disease

***Rickettsia*:** a group of bacteria that act like viruses in the way they attack human cells. They cause a number of diseases, such as Rocky Mountain spotted fever and typhus.

RNA (ribonucleic acid): molecules in the nucleus of a cell that control the cell's chemical activities

salmonella: a group of bacteria that cause food poisoning, intestinal inflammation, typhoid fever, or septicemia (blood poisoning)

smallpox: an often fatal infectious disease marked by chills, high fever, and pus-filled blisters; eradicated worldwide since 1980

statistical association: a finding by an epidemiologic study of an increased number of cases of a disease or condition within a selected population who share one or more characteristics

severe acute respiratory syndrome (SARS): a serious respiratory illness transmitted person to person and caused by a coronavirus originating in Asia in 2003

tularemia: a highly infectious disease caused by the *Francisella tularensis* bacterium; also called rabbit fever

vaccine: a preparation of killed or weakened microorganisms that provides protection from a particular disease

viral hemorrhagic fevers (VHFs): a group of viral diseases characterized by sudden onset, fever, aching, and internal bleeding

virologists: scientists who study viruses

virus: the smallest and simplest kind of life-form; a protein shell containing a core of nucleic acid

West Nile virus: a virus that mainly infects birds but that can infect humans, horses, and other animals. The virus is spread by mosquitoes.

zoonosis: a disease, such as SARS, that spreads from animals to humans

SOURCE NOTES

96   Laurie Garrett, *The Coming Plague: Newly Emerging Diseases in a World Out of Balance* (New York: Farrar, Straus, and Giroux, 1994) 583.

114   University of California, "U.S. Scientist Targeting Crows in War Against West Nile Virus," *UC Newsroom,* September 1, 2006, http://www .universityofcalifornia.edu/news/article/8461 (July 16, 2008).

FOR FURTHER READING

BOOKS

Fleisher, Paul. *Parasites: Latching On to a Free Lunch.* Minneapolis: Twenty-First Century Books, 2006.

Goldsmith, Connie. *Influenza: The Next Pandemic?* Minneapolis: Twenty-First Century Books, 2007.

———. *Invisible Invaders: Dangerous Infectious Diseases.* Minneapolis: Twenty-First Century Books, 2006.

———. *Superbugs Strike Back: When Antibiotics Fail.* Minneapolis: Twenty-First Century Books, 2007.

Yancey, Diane. *Tuberculosis.* Rev. ed. Minneapolis: Twenty-First Century Books, 2008.

Zahler, Diane. *The Black Death.* Minneapolis: Twenty-First Century Books, 2009.

WEBSITES

AIDS, Sex & Teens
http://www.avert.org/young.htm
This site offers a wealth of information about AIDS.

A Beef with Beef
http://whyfiles.org/012mad_cow/index.html
This site offers an expanded discussion of mad cow disease, with links to related sites.

Centers for Disease Control and Prevention
http://www.cdc.gov
This site offers information about a wide range of health issues as well as bulletins from the CDC.

INDEX

ABOUT THE AUTHOR

Mark P. Friedlander Jr. has been a trial attorney in Washington, D.C., and northern Virginia for more than forty-five years. As a lawyer, he played a major role in the litigation that followed the swine flu epidemic of 1976 that never occurred and the massive vaccination program that wasn't needed. He is the author of several books, including *The Immune System* and *When Objects Talk,* in the Discovery! series.

PHOTO ACKNOWLEDGMENTS

The images in this book are used with the permission of: CDC/Courtesy of Cynthia Goldsmith, Jacqueline Katz, and Sherif R. Zaki, pp. 1, 5, 112; © Jim Olive/Peter Arnold, Inc, p. 2; © Bettmann/CORBIS, pp. 8, 42, 44, 48; © Tek Image/Photo Researchers, Inc., p. 12; © Rischgitz/Hulton Archive/Getty Images, p. 17; CDC/James Gathany, pp. 22, 120; CDC/Troy Hall, p. 24; © Dr. Gopal Murti/Photo Researchers, Inc., p. 26; © Laura Westlund/Independent Picture Service, p. 27; © Science Photo Library/Photo Researchers, Inc., pp. 30 (left), 31; © Kul Bhatia/Photo Researchers, Inc., p. 30 (right); © Jean-Loup Charmet/Photo Researchers, Inc., p. 32; © Scala/Art Resource, NY, p. 35; © Alfred Pasieka/Photo Researchers, Inc., pp. 38, 62; © London School of Hygiene/Photo Researchers, Inc., p. 51 (left); © Sinclair Stammers/ Photo Researchers, Inc., p. 51 (right); National Archives, p. 53 (185-G-640-A-13); © NIBSC/Photo Researchers, Inc., pp. 59, 82; © L. Stannard/Photo Researchers, Inc., p. 66; AP Photo/George Widman, p. 69; © Scott Camazine/Photo Researchers, Inc., pp. 73, 94 (right); © POOL/AFP/Getty Images, p. 75; AP Photo, p. 77; Courtesy of Dr. Jim Cheek, p. 80; © N.C.I./Science Source/Photo Researchers, Inc., p. 83; © Giacomo Pirozzi/Panos Pictures, p. 86; © James Prince/Photo Researchers, Inc., p. 90; © Volker Steger/Peter Arnold, Inc., p. 93; © Hank Morgan/Photo Researchers, Inc., p. 94 (left); © David Scharf/Peter Arnold, Inc., p. 97; © CSHL Archives/ Peter Arnold, Inc., p. 99; AP Photo/Patrick Aviolat, p. 104; AP Photo/Ron Thomas, p. 108; © Sonny Tumbelaka/AFP/Getty Images, p. 113; AP Photo/Bob Child, p. 115 (left); © Science VU/CDC/Visuals Unlimited, p. 115 (right); © Peter Parks/ AFP/Getty Images, p. 117; © Qilai Shen/Panos Pictures, p. 118.

Front Cover: © Mike Clarke/AFP/Getty Images (main); CDC/Courtesy of Cynthia Goldsmith, Jacqueline Katz, and Sherif R. Zaki (background).